LAMBERT'S RAILWAY MISCELLANY

LAMBERT'S RAILWAY MISCELLANY

Anthony Lambert

EBURY PRESS

3 5 7 9 10 8 6 4 2

Ebury Press, an imprint of Ebury Publishing,
20 Vauxhall Bridge Road,
London SW1V 2SA

Ebury Press is part of the Penguin Random House group of companies
whose addresses can be found at global.penguinrandomhouse.com

Penguin
Random House
UK

First published by Ebury Press in 2010
This edition published by Ebury Press in 2015

www.eburypublishing.co.uk

A CIP catalogue record for this book is available from the British Library

ISBN 9781785032219

Designed by Peter Ward
Cover by David Wardle
Printed and bound in Great Britain by Clays Ltd, St Ives PLC

MIX
Paper from
responsible sources
FSC
www.fsc.org
FSC® C018179

Penguin Random House is committed to a sustainable future
for our business, our readers and our planet. This book is
made from Forest Stewardship Council® certified paper.

CONTENTS

INTRODUCTION

THIS BOOK IS for those who can relate to the time when most young boys grew up wanting to be an engine driver, for those who remember the atmosphere of moments like those described in Edward Thomas's celebrated poem 'Adlestrop'. It is also for those who are susceptible to the pleasures of any railway journey, encapsulated by Lisa St Aubin de Terán in *Off the Rails* and Edna St Vincent Millay's feeling that 'there isn't a train that I wouldn't take, no matter where it's going'. (Millay was the first woman to receive the Pulitzer Prize for Poetry, and admittedly she died in 1950 before the end of the steam railway and its evocative ambience.)

I grew up towards the end of the steam age, relishing the sight of steam trains on the four-track main line in a cutting at the foot of our garden in Warwickshire. Pocket money was saved for train tickets to railway centres and engine sheds with their captivating aromas of hot oil, steam and coal. A request to look round a shed was hardly ever refused by shedmasters. Most railwaymen took the view that a child's interest in their industry and its mysteries should be met with encouragement. There is a photograph taken between the wars of points being relaid at a London & North Eastern Railway junction with a steam crane at work; in the foreground with their back to the camera and standing right beside the track are an inspector and a knot of fascinated schoolboys. The picture was even taken by the railway's official photographer, reflecting the tacit approval of a benign approach to youthful curiosity.

While at school in Gloucestershire, I spent hours talking to signalmen, whose time between trains allowed them to read and become knowledgeable about all manner of subjects. Gradually I absorbed the fundamentals of mechanical signalling and was allowed to operate the box for an afternoon, the signalman simply writing the bell codes and times in the train register.

That great writer about transport and industry, the late L.T.C. Rolt, thought the appeal of railways could be explained partly by their resolution of the romantic and classical ideals: the desire for freedom and romance implicit in travel complemented by the need for order and discipline; the recognition that the majestic sight of an overnight sleeping car train leaving a cavernous train shed among myriad coloured signal lights is underpinned by one of the most complex organisations devised by man. Each person is part of a hierarchy of interdependent tasks, each vital to the efficient and safe operation of trains.

Railways, although not as individualistic as 50 years ago, are still the antithesis of the bland. Planes and even cars are much the same the world over, homogenised products of international conglomerates. But each country has many different types of train and locomotive, and even if electric or diesel traction does nothing for you, railways offer one of the richest legacies of civic architecture.

But for many it is simply the pleasure of train travel itself that has helped to foster the second railway age, as most countries expand urban networks and build new high-speed lines to reduce our carbon footprint and reliance on fossil fuels. A train journey is an opportunity to work, read, sleep or just gaze out of the window at the passing view. As the renowned poet of the railway, John Betjeman, remarked, trains were made for meditation.

The stories and anecdotes in this book have been chosen in the hope that they will appeal not only to railway buffs but to those who neither know nor care to know the difference between a 'Royal Scot' and a 'Jubilee'.

They rely on no technical knowledge to appreciate the point or humour. Railways have long been fertile ground for farcical or comic situations, and if the majority of stories come from the steam age, that is simply because it was imbued with greater character and characters.

CHAPTER ONE

EARLY DAYS

WHEN THE Stockton & Darlington Railway opened in 1825, no previous invention had had such an impact on mankind as the railway was to have. It not only shrank the world and gave individuals unprecedented mobility, it opened up new markets for goods and liberated early factories from locations dependent on water power. The advent of the railway was greeted with optimism by some, scepticism by others and bewilderment by most, though its potential to transform society was quickly grasped by prescient minds. In a history of the English railway published in 1851, John Francis wrote that by the 1840s 'the possibilities and advantages which the country was to attain with liberal railway communication were deemed to be boundless'. Other countries were not so enthusiastic: the first railway in China, built under the auspices of Jardine Matheson and opened in 1876, was bought up by the Chinese and promptly closed, its four Ipswich-built locomotives and all equipment dumped in Taiwan as though they were a bacillus.

FEAR AND APPREHENSION

Irrational and ignorant fear of railways, and even of the idea of rapid human movement through the air, was expressed in column inches by the mile during the first two decades of railway development. Mrs Gamp in Dickens's *Martin Chuzzlewit* was typical in attributing afflictions to railway travel, and it was commonly thought that those of a nervous disposition would experience suicidal delirium. Tunnels were particularly feared, leading the Liverpool & Manchester Railway to paint the walls of the tunnel at Edge Hill white and illuminate it with gas lights.

Equally widespread was anxiety about the impact of railways and mass transport on society. When the Provost of Eton College, Francis Hodgson, wrote in 1833 that 'no public good whatever could possibly come from such an undertaking', you have the feeling he wasn't simply referring to the Great Western Railway's plan to build a branch to Windsor. The Duke of Wellington put it more bluntly when he described third-class facilities as 'a breach of contract, a premium to the lower orders to go uselessly about the country'.

SURVEYING CONFRONTATIONS

The attitude of most landowners to the idea of railways softened remarkably quickly, outright hostility turning to co-operation and occasionally public-spirited generosity. Most of course welcomed the compensation payments, which exceeded the going rate for farmland. But a small number remained obdurate, causing some lively scenes when surveyors tried to carry out their task. One such was the Earl of Harborough of Stapleford Park in Leicestershire, who so opposed the idea of anyone setting foot on his land that he was even in dispute with the Cottesmore and Belvoir hunts. The prospect of railway surveyors sizing up his acres prompted notices warning them that trespass would be resisted by force. This warning shot was made when the Midland Railway proposed in 1844 a line between Syston and Peterborough, to be laid out by George Stephenson. The 'Battle of Saxby', as it became known, had begun.

The first party of surveyors was met by a group of Lord Harborough's men led by a keeper named Biddle. When threatened with a pistol, he coolly responded, 'Shoot away', but successfully applied for a warrant against the surveyor. Others were arrested and taken by armed escort to Cold Overton Hall to await the local magistrate, but when he was unavailable they were moved on to Leicester Gaol by cart. When this overturned, several surveyors were able to escape. The following day both sides squared up for a full-blooded confrontation: navvies had been added to the railwaymen, and Lord Harborough had drafted in additional men to man the barricades he had erected. Inevitably fists flew before the police arrived and threatened to arrest anyone indulging in further affray. Under cover of the main assault, some surveyors had managed to get into the grounds but were discovered and had their equipment confiscated by the Earl.

The MR suggested a truce while the dispute was settled by a magistrate, who then enjoyed greater jurisdiction than his 21st-century counterpart. The Earl would have none of it, formed a mounted unit using the estate's heavy horses and positioned cannon from his yacht on the Oakham Canal towpath. The battle reached its climax on 16 November, when a diversionary attack along the towpath allowed over a hundred men to survey a substantial area before the mounted unit got to them. A lock-keeper (the Earl had shares in the canal) had enough boxing skills to lay out several railwaymen, and sticks, staves and cudgels produced many injuries on both sides before the railway party withdrew, leaving the Earl's forces with several captives who were released after their details were taken.

In court the following year six railway employees were convicted of causing a riot and imprisoned for one month with a shilling (5p) fine. The Earl was found guilty of causing assault, wrongful imprisonment and causing damage to a railway theodolite, for which he was ordered to pay £8.

Further outbreaks of violence later that year prompted the railway to change the route, taking the line south of the park and hiding it in a shallow tunnel. Work started on this route, but the tunnel collapsed. The only alternative was to build north of the park; hence the great arc that trains still describe around Stapleford Park, although the curve has been eased since the Earl's death.

EVICTING A CONTRACTOR

In 1849 a young assistant of Isambard Kingdom Brunel, Robert Marchant, asked to be released to go into partnership with a man named Williams with a view to building Mickleton Tunnel on the Oxford, Worcester & Wolverhampton Railway. The OWW, for which Brunel was the engineer, came to be dubbed the 'Old Worse and Worse', with good reason. Construction began, but a financial crisis brought all work to a halt for over a year. Litigation ensued over the terms of the contract, souring relations to such a degree that the OWW accepted an offer from another contractor, Peto & Betts, to finish building the entire line, including Mickleton Tunnel.

Williams & Marchant refused to budge from the construction site and drove off attempts to take it. On one occasion the Riot Act was read. Brunel decided on overwhelming force. On the evening of 20 July 1851 men began assembling in Evesham, Fenny Compton, Charlbury, Harbury and Cheltenham. By midnight seven or eight brigades of about 250 men each had converged on Chipping Campden, near the tunnel workings. Marchant was forewarned and had sent for Captain Lefroy and the police stationed in Cheltenham as well as local magistrates. By 5am on Monday, Marchant's 150 navvies were hopelessly outnumbered by Brunel's force of about 2,000. There was little Lefroy's police force of 30 could do but look on. A Peto & Betts man carrying pistols was disarmed, though it would appear Marchant was similarly prepared.

Brunel's solicitor and a magistrate taking Marchant's side parleyed, and a document was signed agreeing to put the matter to arbitration. Brunel offered employment for Marchant's navvies and to leave the site if the matter went against him. This settlement enabled Lefroy to halt a body of troops coming from Coventry. It is hard to know how much violence actually occurred; the reports of eyewitnesses in regional papers suggest *The Times*'s account of the altercation was exaggerated. It reported dislocated shoulders, broken heads and a missing finger, whereas others thought the violence was of 'a very slight description'.

PIONEERS IN THE GOWER

The world's very first railway passenger service was operated by what became the Swansea & Mumbles Railway in South Wales, which opened on 25 March 1807 between Swansea and Oystermouth. It was extraordinary in using at various times no fewer than eight different forms of power: horse, compressed air, steam, battery, petrol, diesel, overhead electric and, on one occasion at least, sail. The last double-deck, 106-seat tram ran on 5 January 1960.

THE PERILS OF RAILWAY CONSTRUCTION IN AFRICA

You needed great optimism and a lot of luck to survive the rigours of railway construction in some parts of Africa. When the Beira Railway in Mozambique was being built in the early 1890s, even the construction site near the coast at Fontesvilla was fraught with risk. It was situated in the crocodile-infested swamps of the Pungwe delta, so buildings had to be raised above ground and clouds of mosquitoes filled the air. The contractor, George Pauling, was convinced that alcohol warded off fever and lived by the idea; during a three-day inspection of the line with two other men, about 300 pints of beer were drunk. The only antidote for malaria was quinine, which had to be taken in large revolting flakes. Whatever the reality, drinking was ruinously expensive, a tot of whisky that would cost 4d (1.3p) in England setting you back 10s 6d (52½p) in Beira.

Mortality was so high that arriving European staff had to choose a gravestone from a selection in Pauling's headquarters and compose their own epitaph. If a man survived the full term of his contract, he would ceremonially break up the stone. The chief engineer, Arthur Lawley, weighed 210 pounds (95 kg) at the beginning of the work and just 140 lb (63.5 kg) by its conclusion. Even Pauling, who won a wager that he could carry a 450 lb (205 kg) pony around a billiard table, succumbed to malaria and dysentery – despite his intake of alcohol.

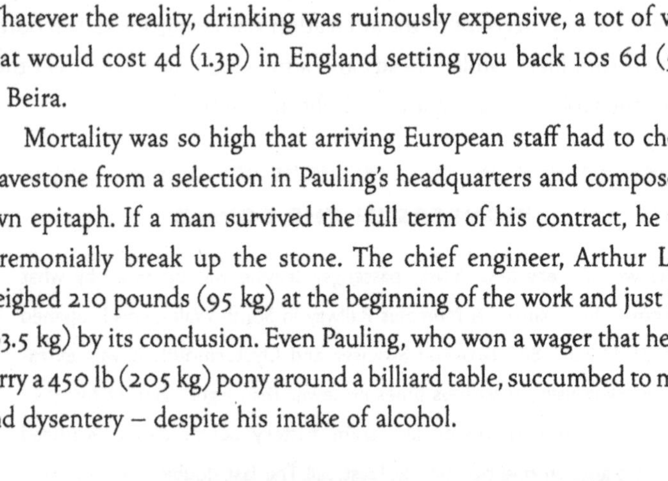

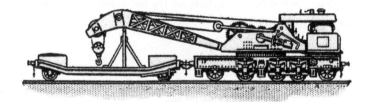

A EUREKA MOMENT

The congregation at St George's Church in Tredegar in the early 19th century had an unexpected and doubtless shocking interruption one Sunday. One of its members was the industrialist Samuel Homfray, proprietor of the local ironworks, who was grappling with the problems of building the Sirhowy Tramroad, which opened in 1805. Rather than attending to spiritual matters, he was using the sand on the church floor as a sketch-pad for devising a means of diverting wagons from one track to another. Suddenly he hit upon a solution and shouted, 'Damn it. I've got it!' The point, or switch in US parlance, was born.

OPENING BANQUETS

For many places the opening of a railway line has been the most seismic event in their history, and one to be celebrated on a grand scale whenever possible. After the formal opening ceremony, it became usual to hold a day of celebrations involving the populations of the towns served by the railway and an elaborate banquet for selected guests in a suitable hotel.

An unusually altruistic occasion was the opening of the Buckinghamshire Railway between Verney Junction and Oxford on 20 May 1851. As chairman of the railway company, Sir Harry Verney of Claydon House (now in the care of the National Trust) arranged an excursion for 280 Ragged School children and their teachers from Westminster to Islip. On arrival at the 18th-century mansion, the children tucked into a lunch of 'meat, plum pudding and apple pies. Beer was also supplied; but a great number of the children being teetotallers declined it and preferred water.' The afternoon was spent in games and exploring the grounds.

The august contractor Thomas Brassey laid on a banquet for 250 guests for the opening of the North Staffordshire Railway branch from Rocester to Ashbourne, on 31 May 1852. The *Staffordshire Advertiser* detailed the fare consumed: 'Baron of beef, 16 dishes potted trout, 16 ditto pickled salmon, 52 lobsters, 10 pigeon pies, 42 couple roast chickens, 6 turkeys, 10 quarters lamb, 8 haunches mutton, 16 pieces ribs beef, 10 ditto boiled ditto, 24 tongues, 8 hams, 12 joints veal, 6 venison pasties, 6 savoury pies, 12 couple boiled chickens, 2 couple guinea fowls, jellies, custards, blancmanges, lemon cheese cake, Bakewell puddings, rhubarb tarts, preserve ditto, hunting puddings. – Dessert, grapes, oranges, gingerbread, figs, and sponge-cakes.'

Even local railways would celebrate the opening in a hotel along the line, though some could not afford to foot the bill. When the Dursley & Midland Junction Railway opened in 1856, anyone attending the celebratory dinner had to pay for themselves. Nor were the surroundings always conducive to comfort: when the Dingwall & Skye Railway was opened on 7 September 1870, the draughty wooden train shed at Strome Ferry was the setting for the banquet for 470 people, catered for by the Peacock Hotel in Inverness.

One of the last grand openings was that of the Great Central Railway from Nottingham to London Marylebone. Guests travelled in three special trains from Manchester, Sheffield and Nottingham on 9 March 1899. A six-course lunch was served to about 734 in a specially erected marquee on the concourse at Marylebone. A military band played a largely Germanic programme which included Brahms, Wagner and Strauss. Unfortunately, no record appears to have survived about the logistics of feeding so many in the days before gas cylinders. It is possible that the kitchens of the Hotel Great Central (now the Landmark Hotel) were useable, but the hotel was certainly not finished. The honour of opening the last main line into London was given to the head of the Board of Trade, the Rt. Hon. C.T. Ritchie, who in his speech spoke of the need for additional capacity for traffic into London from the north – anticipating exactly the argument behind the 2010 plans for a corresponding high-speed line.

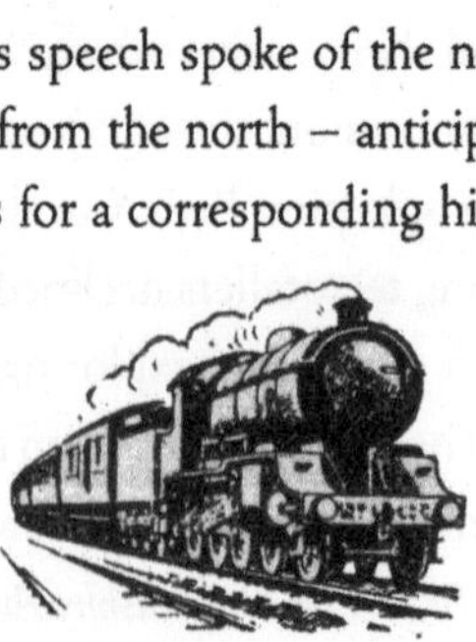

FOUR-LEGGED FRIENDS

The most useless if popular member of the station staff at London Paddington was a cat named Tiddles, who was adopted in 1970 as a six-week-old kitten by the ladies' lavatory attendant June Watson. She took him home one day, thinking he would like a conventional domain, but Tiddles much preferred to snooze in a corner of the station lavatory. The reason became all too apparent as the fat cat enjoyed a high-fat, high-calorie diet of chicken livers, kidneys, rabbit and steak brought in by admirers and kept in his personal fridge. Dealing with mice or rats like any self-respecting station cat was the last thing on Tiddles' mind; all he could take on was other feline fatties, winning the 1982 London Fat Cat Championship, weighing in at 30lb (13.6kg). Tiddles had gained another 2lb (0.9kg) by the time he was put to sleep the following year, killed by kindness.

PAPAL CHOIRS

In France, for the opening of the Paris–Strasbourg line in 1852, four locomotives on parallel lines approached a canopied dais to receive the blessing of the Archbishop of Strasbourg. Napoleon III himself would be present at the more important openings to signify his support for the development of railways. Even more fantastic ceremonies were laid on in Italy: the opening ceremony of the first railway in the Papal States, from

Rome to Velletri, was supposed to be performed by the reformist Pope Pius IX, who had authorised railway construction, but bad weather prevented his attendance. His chaplain, the Archbishop Prince of Hohenlohe, blessed the locomotive and train, surrounded by prelates of the Apostolic Court and the musicians of the Sistine Chapel. Regiments from France (the railway was built by a French company) and Rome formed the guard of honour.

MANUAL LUBRICATION S&D-STYLE

The chaldron wagons found on the primitive wagonways of the North East coalfield naturally became the first wagons of the Stockton & Darlington Railway. Their crude inside bearings made it impossible for them to make the journey between Shildon and Stockton without gradually slowing. To avoid losing time, the locomotive crew resorted to the dangerous expedient of jumping off the engine on opposite sides, once the train had slowed to walking pace, and giving the bearings on each wagon a brush of oil. Normally they could run to get back on the engine, but sometimes the lubrication had immediate effect and they had to jump on the last wagon and make their way forward over the coals.

RIGHT OF PASSAGE

Superintending the anarchic traffic in the early years of the Stockton & Darlington Railway must have been a nightmare. Steam power shared the track with horse-drawn trains. It was a single line with four passing places per mile but had no signalling system, and the traffic manager, John Graham, had to contend with six 'open access' coach operators in addition to the mineral traffic. It was soon evident that horses and steam locomotives were like oil and water, and the Shildon locomotive drivers – 'not the most manageable class of beings' in Robert Stephenson's estimation – regarded themselves as top dogs. The rule was that if two trains met, whichever was past the half-way post between loops should have the right of way. Graham had to deal with such incidents as three horse-drivers abandoning their train for a two-hour drinking session in a nearby pub, horse-drivers refusing to let a steam locomotive overtake them at a loop, and drivers simply ignoring the post rule. The nadir came when two rip-roaring drunk horse-drivers tore up track by racing along with a derailed wagon, forced another driver into a loop and overturned his empty wagons, and finally ripped out a rail rather than give way to a steam locomotive.

YOU WANT A *SEAT*?

Early third- and even second-class carriages had neither roofs nor windows, and sides might be little more than thigh high. Holes were drilled in the floor to drain rainwater. Within a year of the Liverpool & Manchester Railway opening in 1830, it had received complaints from passengers that clothes had been set on fire by sparks from locomotives, so it was agreed that 'tops' should be fitted, of either painted canvas or wood. The question of whether seats should be provided was neatly solved by the Chester & Birkenhead Railway, which created a fourth class without them. The *Railway Times* opined that 'we do not feel disposed to attach much weight to the argument in favour of third class carriages with seats. [Providing nothing was done] to hurt the feelings of those who may use these inferior vehicles . . . we do not think that the public have any just ground to murmur.'

As late as 1888, a lady travelling on the Cambrian Railways boarded a carriage which 'astounded me, for I thought this kind of thing had long ago been turned into tool-sheds for London suburban gardens'.

RAILWAY SIGNS

Seen on Agra station, India, in the 1990s:

'THE TIME INDICATED ON THE TIMETABLE IS NOT THE TIME AT WHICH THE TRAIN WILL LEAVE; IT IS THE TIME BEFORE WHICH THE TRAIN WILL DEFINITELY NOT LEAVE.'

THE FIRST FATALITY

It was a cruel irony that the first fatality on a steam railway should have been William Huskisson and that it should have been on the opening day of the Liverpool & Manchester Railway, of which he had been a keen supporter. Huskisson was MP for Liverpool and President of the Board of Trade. The accident happened on 15 September 1830 at Parkside, where the cavalcade of eight trains halted and Huskisson got out of his carriage to talk to the Duke of Wellington, only to be surprised by the

Rocket, which knocked him down and crushed his leg. Huskisson was placed in a carriage hauled by the best locomotive, *Northumbrian*, which had been driven by George Stephenson in the cavalcade, and taken to Eccles at 36 mph (58 kph), but he died that night.

BOYS FOR MEN'S WORK

The work of the steam locomotive fireman is arduous, requiring the shovelling of several tons of coal during a shift. During 1833 the Liverpool & Manchester Railway, in its third year of operation, was taking a scythe to costs despite good financial results. One of its most ignominious and foolish economies was the replacement of adult firemen by boys at lower wages. The company allowed the firemen to remain at their posts until they had found alternative employment. Within a decade the boot would be on the other foot, as the demand for competent drivers and firemen exceeded supply, following a spate of railway openings.

BEFORE DINING-CARS

For those passengers who did not bring food to sustain them on a journey, railway companies stopped trains at certain places for the hasty consumption of a meal, sometimes pre-ordered. One of the first stations to provide this service was Wolverton on the London & Birmingham Railway, where passengers were fortified by a staff of 28 from 7.30am to the departure of the York mail train at about 11pm. A freelance journalist, Francis Head, left an account of the arrival of a train: '. . . youthful handmaidens stand in a row behind bright silver urns, silver coffee pots, silver tea pots, cups, saucers, cakes, sugar, milk, with other delicacies over which they preside, the confused crowd of passengers simultaneously liberated from the train hurry towards with them with a velocity exactly proportionate to their appetites.'

At Tonbridge, where South Eastern Railway passengers disgorged, it was common for the passengers to be recalled to the train almost as soon as they had received their coffee, compelling them to leave it undrunk and speculate how many times a cup of coffee could be resold. Charles Dickens lampooned refreshment rooms in the short story 'Mugby Junction', leaving little doubt of the place he had in mind in writing it – Rugby.

On the Midland Railway a table d'hôte menu was handed out after the train left St Pancras. At Leicester orders were given to staff who telegraphed them to Normanton in Yorkshire, where soup would be on the table as passengers poured into the dining-room. Just 20 minutes were allowed for the stop. The Midland emerged with the best reputation for its dining-rooms and dining-cars.

EARLY PHILANTHROPY

The bonded stores of railway companies took samples of wines and spirits in their care, which remained the property of the railway company. The directors of the Liverpool & Manchester Railway generously decided to donate this liquor, which amounted to a substantial volume in a year, to the infirmaries of the two cities 'for the benefit of the patients'.

SNOUTS IN THE TROUGH

In the lecture on 'Merrie England' delivered by Jim Dixon in *Lucky Jim*, Kingsley Amis satirises the tendency of every generation to think they have been born too late to enjoy a golden age of probity and goodwill. A corrective is provided by the trials of operating the Liverpool & Manchester Railway in 1833, when there appears to have been an epidemic of dishonesty in all quarters. Parcels either went missing or were pilfered in transit and at depots. Coal was liberally removed from wagons, and a parcel containing 30 sovereigns and a £5 note arrived with nothing more than a few coppers. Matters at the Market Street office in Manchester were so bad that every member of staff was transferred to a different post and new men were brought in.

To begin with, permanent way men were paid on a piecework system. It was discovered that much of their time was spent generating work for themselves by smashing up the mix of stone blocks and wood baulks that acted as sleepers to which the rails were fastened.

Part of the problem may have lain with the laxness of procedures in what was still an entirely new form of commercial organisation. For example, it was normal practice for the porter charged with locking up the booking office at Crown Street, Liverpool, to take home for safe-keeping the day's takings in a tin box.

INDIGNITIES IN LEICESTERSHIRE

Railway openings did not always go according to plan. When the historic Leicester & Swannington Railway was opened on 17 July 1832, with George Stephenson himself driving the inaugural train, there were more than red faces. As the only closed carriage was the directors' saloon, even the Mayor of Leicester and other important guests had to make do with open wagons.

All went well until half-way through the narrow bore of the 1 mile (1.6 km) long Glenfield Tunnel, when there was a jolt and the train came to an abrupt halt. The bandsmen, who had been struggling to play in the dark, were thrown about and gave up. It transpired that platelayers had inadvertently raised the track when repairing a broken rail, and the locomotive's chimney had fouled the tunnel roof and broken off. When the train emerged from the tunnel, it made an unscheduled stop for the passengers to wash their faces in a lineside brook.

DISPOSING OF *ROCKET*

Two years after the Stephensons' *Rocket* won the 1829 Rainhill Trials to determine the motive power for the Liverpool & Manchester Railway, the LMR directors were approached by Haydock Collieries with a view to buying it. The directors declined to sell, not because of any historical value but because the railway did not have enough locomotives. After acting as a test bed for a rotary steam engine designed by Lord Dundonald in 1834, *Rocket* was sold to J. Thompson, lessee of the Earl of Carlisle's collieries and lime works in Cumberland, which were served by Lord Carlisle's own railway system. It was claimed that soon after her arrival, *Rocket* was used during a fiercely contested election and covered the distance of over 4½ miles (7.2 km) between Midgeholme and Kirkhouse in 4½ minutes.

In 1862 the historic locomotive was donated by the Thompsons, then of Milton Hall near Brampton in Cumberland, to the Patent Office

Museum in London. In 1883 *Rocket*, together with all the other items in its collection, was transferred to the Science Museum, where it can be seen today.

The London & North Western Railway (which became owner of the LMR) built a replica of *Rocket*, which was displayed at London's White City before the First World War.

CATERING FOR SMOKERS

The railway companies were reluctant to cater for smokers. This had nothing to do with the health issues that have prompted the modern ban on smoking in trains and on railway premises. It was concern with the fire risk at stations and with the stink (as Dr Johnson would have it) on upholstery in first-class carriages. As there was none to be polluted in early second- and third-class carriages, smoking was tolerated there. In 1840 a suggestion was made that 'a carriage should be placed at the end of the train, after the private carriages mounted on trucks, so that the smell of the smoke would be left behind as the train proceeded, and no travellers would be inconvenienced by the tobacco fumes.'

Such grudging provision for smokers came to an end in 1868, when the Regulation of Railways Act (supported by John Stuart Mill) stipulated that a smoking carriage must be attached to every train containing more than one carriage of each class, unless the Board of Trade allowed a derogation. Carriages were labelled 'Smoking' except for those on the South Eastern & Chatham Railway which used the later style of 'Non-smoking'.

SPARKS TO THE GIANT'S CAUSEWAY

The famous Giant's Causeway in Northern Ireland was once linked to the broad-gauge railway at Portrush by a 3 ft gauge electric tramway. As one of the earliest electric railways in the world, opening in 1883, it attracted engineers from all over the globe. The current was generated by a hydro-electric power plant where the dynamos were controlled by one man sitting on a chair in front of an ammeter and a large wheel. When the ammeter indicated increased current flow through movement of a train, he simply turned the wheel to increase the water flow to the turbines. The driver of the first tram of the day also delivered the newspapers to properties alongside the track by opening the window of his cab and, without stopping and through long practice, flinging them into the gardens.

GRAND OPENING

When the light railway was opened between The Mound and Dornoch on the east coast of Scotland in June 1902, the general manager of the Highland Railway, Thomas Wilson, described the occasion as 'a red-letter day in the history of the empire!'

TRIALS OF EARLY TRAVEL

Early steam locomotives relied upon a pump to force water into the boiler to be turned into steam; later, steam was used to force water into the boiler through injectors. Until the injector's invention, passengers were sometimes delayed when pumps failed to replenish the water level at a sufficient rate. When this happened, the locomotive had to be uncoupled from the train and run up and down the line about a dozen times before being recoupled to the train. The rate of water consumption is naturally higher when the locomotive is pulling a train, so simply continuing its journey without restoring a safe water level was not an option.

AN ECCENTRIC EARLY WRITER

One of the most extraordinary characters of the early 19th century was Dr Dionysius Lardner (1793–1859), son of a Dublin solicitor. Despite being a professor of natural philosophy at the University of London, editor of the 133-volume *Cabinet Cyclopaedia* and meriting a mention in Marx's *Das Kapital*, he made some absurdly wild prophecies about the impact of railway travel, for which he was ridiculed. Amongst his more absurd notions was that 'rail travel at high speed is not possible because passengers, unable to breathe, would die of asphyxia'.

Lardner's career in England came to an unlikely end in 1841, when he ran off to Paris with the wife of Captain Richard Heaviside. The irate Dragoon Guard pursued the couple and gave Lardner a flogging, to no avail. The couple were married in 1846, four years before publication of *Railway Economy*, in which Lardner made a contribution to railway management by highlighting the value of statistical evidence in making decisions. He died in Naples and was buried in the English Cemetery.

WHAT'S IN A NAME?

One of the first railways in Russia was built to enable the Tsar and his family to visit the 600-hectare pleasure grounds at Pavlovsk on the outskirts of St Petersburg. The terminus there was a sufficiently grand affair to be used for concerts and dances. The name of the best-known pleasure grounds in London, Vauxhall (itself derived from the 13th-century owner of the area, Faulke de Breaute – Faulke's Hall), was attached to the Russian park, and Vokzal is still Russian for a railway station.

INVENTOR OF THE FISHPLATE

Another eccentric character from the early days of railways was William Bridges Adams (1797–1872), whose main claim to fame was his invention of the fishplate, an elongated rectangle of iron used in pairs to join together two rails – one of the most crucial fittings used on railways the world over. Poor health compelled him to live in Chile until he was 40, returning in 1837. Six years later he set up the Fairfield Works in Bow,

London – which later became the Bryant & May match factory and scene of one of the seminal strikes in British labour history, the matchgirls' strike of 1888. There, Adams devised a series of inventions and built steam railcars. His 1862 book, *Roads and Rails, and their sequences, physical and moral*, fizzes with ideas on all manner of subjects from food preservation to clothes – he detested buttons and tight-fitting clothes, so invented different fastenings.

SEE THE CONQUERING HERO COME

It was perfectly normal for the church to be involved with opening ceremonies in some, usually Catholic, countries. Secular speeches about progress were more in line with British sensibilities, but an exception was the cutting of the first sod of the Hull & Barnsley Railway, when the ecclesiastical authorities were involved. The railway had been promoted to break the stranglehold of the North Eastern Railway on the Humber city's trade, and the directors decided to make a carnival of the occasion, on Saturday 15 January 1881. Stands were erected for 7,000 spectators, 4,870 of them invited guests, and 400 spaces were reserved for miners from the south Yorkshire collieries which the railway would serve. Church bells were rung, cannons fired and a great procession converged on the dock site, where a choir of 2,000 accompanied by 12 bands sang a song specially commissioned from the Rev. Kemp of Hull Charterhouse. Its last verse ran:

Once more the shout, for we are free,
By no monopoly confined,
To work our town's high destiny,
The lot by Providence designed.
Fair field, no favour, our demand;
Fair field, no favour, has been won.
Thanks to the chief and gallant band,
By whom the glorious feat was done.
God's love and grace on all our labours shine,
God fill our Dock with ships, God speed the line!

In the evening there were bonfires and fireworks and a gala performance of Hengler's Circus. Of course many of the spectators arrived by North Eastern Railway trains.

BRUNEL'S FIASCO

One of Brunel's few failures was his choice, for the South Devon Railway, of the atmospheric system of train propulsion whereby stationary pumping engines created a vacuum in front of a piston in a tube between the rails. The piston was connected to the train by a cranked plate emerging through a slot in the tube. This had to be sealed by a greased leather flap, but the grease attracted rats to eat the leather, affecting the vacuum. The system was invented by Joseph Samuda, who was rash enough to claim that the 53-mile (85 km) journey between Exeter and Plymouth might be reduced to half an hour – requiring an average speed of 106 mph (170 kph). Atmospheric trains were operated between Exeter and Newton Abbot, but the only main-line application of the system was a failure, and conventional locomotives took over from 6 September 1848. The railway itself has been both blessed and cursed by the delightful stretch along the sea wall between Starcross and Teignmouth;

it is one of the loveliest sections of railway in the world, but a nightmare for the civil engineers. Soon after the line opened between Exeter and Teignmouth on 30 May 1846, a gale drove a ship ashore at Powderham with its bowsprit so obstructing the line that it was cut in two by a train.

BY DUCAL APPOINTMENT

It was not unusual for railway stations close to a landed seat to have at least a private waiting room, but a standard-gauge railway built to connect an estate was rare. One such was the Wotton Tramway built by the Duke of Buckingham to connect his Wotton estate with the Aylesbury & Buckingham Railway at Quainton Road. Apart from a short stretch, the 4¼-mile (6.8 km) line was built entirely on his own land using estate workers. It opened in 1871 and was later extended to Brill, becoming known as the Brill Tramway. To add to its landed connections, there was a branch to the Waddesdon Manor gasworks of Lord Rothschild.

HIGHLAND RESTITUTION

The 3rd Duke of Sutherland, perhaps in penance or at least out of a sense of righting a wrong for the Highland Clearances carried out in the name of his grandfather, spent colossal sums creating new employment opportunities in the county, one of which was the Duke of Sutherland's Railway between Golspie and Helmsdale. Besides owning this 17-mile (27 km) line, the Duke was the principal shareholder in the Sutherland & Caithness Railway, which built the rest of the line north to Wick and Thurso. He had also been instrumental in building the first line into the Highlands, from Perth to Inverness, through buying a princely £355,545 worth of shares in the Inverness & Perth Junction Railway.

The 3rd Duke was passionate about mechanical matters. There are stories of him and the Prince of Wales following the then steam-powered fire engines to a blaze when in London, but it was on the Highland Railway that he was able to indulge himself. He had Kitson of Leeds build a tank engine, named *Dunrobin* after his castle, to operate his railway until the HR took over the railway, after which the locomotive continued to be kept at Brora to haul the Duke over the 86 miles (138 km) to Inverness for board meetings.

The 4th Duke inherited something of his father's partiality for mechanical matters and asked David Jones, the Highland's locomotive superintendent, to design a new locomotive. The handsome 0–4–4 tank built by Sharp, Stewart in Glasgow, also named *Dunrobin*, was kept in a shed at Golspie with a small four-wheel day saloon to take the Duke to Inverness and other places on the HR. A much grander saloon running on bogies was built in 1899 at Wolverton with overnight accommodation for longer journeys south from Inverness; the coach was kept in a shed close to the private station at the end of the drive to Dunrobin Castle. Today it can be admired at the National Railway Museum in York.

The cab of *Dunrobin* had panels removed from the earlier locomotive on which distinguished guests signed their names; they included Queen Alexandra, George V, Kaiser Wilhelm II, Edward VII and Neville

Chamberlain. *Dunrobin* was loaned to the HR for shunting during the First World War, and during the Second was used for the same purpose at Invergordon, Rosyth and Dalmuir. In 1949 *Dunrobin* and the day saloon were sold, since British Railways wasn't having private engines running around its nationalised lines. They ended up at New Romney in Kent in the care of Captain J.E.P. Howey, who had built the Romney Hythe & Dymchurch Railway. After 15 years there, they were sold to a private buyer in British Columbia and are today displayed at Fort Steele Heritage Town.

EMBELLISHING THE LINE

Where railways were built through landed estates, a quid pro quo might be the decoration of a bridge or tunnel portal. Bridge No. 69 on the London & North Western Railway between Rugby and Long Buckby has ornamental cast-iron railings ending in scrollwork 'armchairs' or alcoves, which gave the bridge its nickname of the 'pulpit bridge'. It was erected to a design approved by Lord Henley, whose arms were incorporated in the 'pulpits'. Also on the LNWR, the Earl of Lichfield exacted a magnificent stone bridge to carry the railway over the Lichfield Drive within Shugborough Park. Its low elliptical arch is flanked by paired Ionic columns and curved balustraded wing walls, with the Earl's arms placed on a central plinth. Both portals to Shugborough Tunnel also received unusually elaborate treatment.

CHAPTER TWO

GRAND DESIGNS

BRITAIN GAVE railways to the world, and its engineers and manufacturers were to play a major role in building and equipping railways all over the globe. Perhaps the most extraordinary achievement of the railway builders has been the longevity of their creations. Viaducts and bridges are today carrying trains of a weight and speed that far exceed the calculations of their designers. In many cases they built for aesthetic quality as well as solidity, bequeathing structures that are generally regarded as enhancements to the landscape. Monsal Dale in Derbyshire is one of the most exceptional landscape settings for a railway viaduct, and Ruskin fulminated against the stone-faced five-arch bridge across the River Wye; yet when it was threatened with demolition after closure of the railway in 1968, latter-day environmentalists campaigned successfully to save it and today it forms part of the Monsal Trail. The great 19th-century train sheds that span city platforms are admired as uplifting portals to civilised travel, inducing feelings very different from the Stygian gloom of a 1960s bunker such as Birmingham New Street. Change of the most positive kind has affected tunnel construction: the dreadful conditions endured by 19th-century navvies have been replaced by methods that have allowed such impressive achievements as the Seikan Tunnel in Japan, the Channel Tunnel and the Alpine base tunnels in Switzerland.

THE VALUE OF LIFE IN THE PENNINES

One of the most notorious examples of early Victorian disregard for human life emerged from the inquiry into construction of the first Woodhead Tunnel, built between 1839 and 1845. Even George Stephenson blanched at the idea of building it, remarking that he would eat the first locomotive to go through it. Two of the finest professionals of their day were given the task, Joseph Locke as consultant and Charles Blacker Vignoles as engineer, but there was animosity between them and between Vignoles and the board of the Sheffield, Ashton-under-Lyne & Manchester Railway. A measure of the board's lack of concern for the welfare of the navvies building the 3-mile (4.8 km) tunnel was their reluctance to provide so much as tents for the 400 men sinking the first shaft on the bleak, windswept moorland. The relationship between the board and Vignoles deteriorated to the point of legal action, and in his diary for 15 January 1841, he wrote: 'Good God, that men whom I had served so faithfully and for whose railway I had done so much, should act like this.'

Locke took over. As the number of tunnelling faces rose to 12, navvy numbers grew and conditions deteriorated still further. The western, Woodhead end of the tunnel was so remote that Locke's biographer in 1862 likened the difficulty of victualling the camp with that encountered at Balaclava in the Crimea. The men paid out of their own wages for the services of a doctor from Hollingworth, 8 miles (13 km) away, and he attributed most accidents to the recklessness and drunkenness of the men. News of their brutish state spread, and a missionary was sent to live among them; his journal provides us with details of the men's plight. The heat in the tunnel workings was so great that the men drank the ankle-deep muddy water in which they stood. When navvies were scarce, they were asked to work double and treble shifts, and when many should have been sleeping they were drinking. The casualty lists are incomplete, but at least 32 men were killed and 140 seriously injured. Many of these accidents were caused by the use of iron rather than copper stemmers to pack powder into a drilled hole for blasting, simply because copper ones cost more.

This excessive loss of life, which contemporary Cornish mine engineers regarded as evidence of gross mismanagement, led to an investigation by a Commons Select Committee in 1846. Appearing before it, the engineer W.A. Purdon was asked whether the patent fuse was not safer than those employed, to which he gave the infamous reply: 'Perhaps it is; but it is attended with such a loss of time, and the difference is so very small, I would not recommend the loss of time for the sake of all the extra lives it would save.'

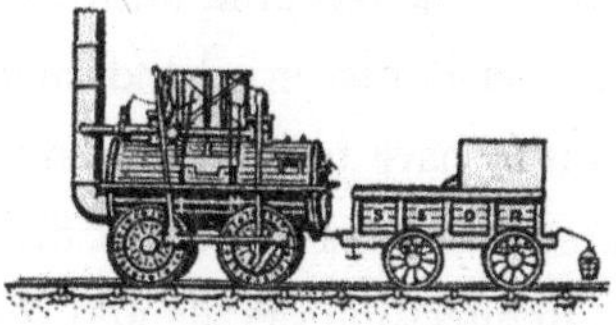

CATHEDRALS OF THE RAILWAY

'This station was built for *human* beings, something to make them feel welcome and exalted ...' These words of Rogers Whitaker (see page 220) referred to the marble columns and terracotta mosaics at Scranton station in Pennsylvania, but the reaction could apply to thousands of stations that lift the spirits and lend a sense of occasion to the basic purpose of travel. Stations on almost every continent were designed with cavernous naves and transepts of iron and glass, married to façades in almost every architectural style.

In Britain, Brunel and Matthew Digby Wyatt would be gratified how little changed London Paddington is from the station they completed in 1854, 'after my own fancy' as Brunel put it. The North Eastern Railway created magnificent curved roofs for its stations at York and Newcastle, the latter graced by John Dobson's façade and Thomas Prosser's portico – and one of very few Grade I-listed railway buildings. London St Pancras is probably the best-loved station, especially now that Gilbert Scott's hotel and station together with W.H. Barlow's train shed have been so triumphantly restored and adapted for a new railway age.

It seems miraculous that an exact copy of the original colossal Dent clockface is able to greet arriving Eurostar passengers. In the 1970s British Rail, with its then customary indifference to heritage, decided to sell the 10 ft (3 m) timepiece but the workmen taking it down dropped it – rather a costly blunder since BR had agreed a sale price of £¼ million. The shattered pieces were bagged up by a railwayman, Roland Hoggard, and taken by train to Nottingham. In his garden at Thrugarton, Hoggard with admirable English eccentricity reassembled the clock and incorporated it into his garden outbuildings. This served as the blueprint for today's clock, replicated with the same Welsh slate numerals, cast-iron hands and gold-leaf decoration.

In the US the laurels have to go to Grand Central in New York, designed by the architectural firms of Reed & Stem (overall design) and Warren & Wetmore (architectural details and the Beaux-Arts style). It was built between 1903 and 1913 over two levels of tracks, originally with 66 on the upper level for long-distance expresses and 57 on the lower for suburban trains. It is famous for its Oyster Bar and for having private retail outlets, rather than chains.

LOST TREASURES

In Britain unquestionably the greatest architectural loss has been Philip Hardwick's Doric Propylaeum, which graced the entrance to the London & Birmingham Railway's station at Euston. Opened in 1838, the Euston Arch represented 'as no other structure in the world the moment of supreme optimism in the marriage of steam and progress', in Sir John Summerson's words. Built of stone from Bramley Fall in Yorkshire, it was the subject of fierce controversy from 1960 when the British Transport Commission announced its intention to demolish it as part of Euston's reconstruction for electric train services. As the *Architectural Review* commented, 'in spite of . . . being one of the outstanding architectural creations of the early nineteenth century and the most important – and visually satisfying – monument to the railway age which Britain pioneered, the united efforts of many organisations and individuals failed to save it in the face of official apathy and philistinism.'

Equivalent philistinism was shown in New York with the destruction in 1963 of the magnificent Beaux-Arts Penn Central station, built between 1906 and 1910. Corner pavilions flanked long classical façades, and the waiting area was a re-creation of Rome's Baths of Caracalla with grand staircases on each side, rising through colonnades under huge arches framed by Corinthian columns. Placing the tracks below ground was made possible by substitution of steam for electric traction at a station named Manhattan Transfer. Designed by McKim, Mead & White, Penn Central was created for 600,000 passengers a day and was regarded as one of the architectural jewels of New York City. As Sir John Summerson said, it was 'a building in which Diocletian and Paxton sublimely met'.

FOUR-LEGGED FRIENDS

It was once quite common for a cuddly dog such as a St Bernard to wander main stations collecting money for good causes, usually by means of a collecting box strapped on to its back. In 1910 Brum II (presumably succeeding Brum I) began collecting money at Euston station for the London & North Western Railway Servants' Benevolent Fund. By 1917 he had collected £1,500. A dog named Carlo from Ryde on the Isle of Wight was a familiar sight at island stations and collected for the orphanage founded in 1885 by the London & South Western Railway.

A CANADIAN QUID PRO QUO

The Canadian Pacific Railway was built to secure the confederation and particularly the adherence of British Columbia through a deal between the government and the CPR: in exchange for about $25 million and 25 million acres (10 million ha) of land, Canada would have a railway link across 2,909 miles (4,680 km) between Montreal and Vancouver. The sale of farmland in lots across the prairie provinces provided an initial income and laid the foundation of the railway's traffic. The first train across the country came to a stand beside Burrard Inlet on the west coast on 23 May 1887 after what was then the world's longest continuous train journey. The locomotive, No. 374, is preserved in Roundhouse Park, Vancouver.

THE GOTTHARD TUNNEL

Work on this 9-mile (15 km) tunnel between Göschenen and Airolo on the main Zürich–Milan line began in June 1872. Louis Favre from Geneva was entrusted with building it. He had gambled that he would construct it in less than the eight years allowed, being paid 5,000 Swiss francs for each day he could save or being penalised by the same amount for each day's delay; Favre thought he could do it in six and make himself a rich man. More than 2,500 men toiled day and night to bore the tunnel, but it was 1880 before the two headings even met, and by that time Favre was buried in the cemetery at Göschenen at the northern end of the tunnel. He had died of a heart attack in the tunnel the previous year, aged just 53. It had always been the intention that Favre, known as Di Capo, should be the first to pass through the opening following the breakthrough; his workmen honoured that by passing through the hole a tin box containing his photograph. A ceremonial opening train travelled through the tunnel on 23 May 1882, after 177 men had died during its construction. Had he lived, Favre would have owed over 2 million Swiss francs.

The Gotthard Tunnel became the principal rail freight artery linking northern and southern Europe, the route's importance reflected in the construction of the 35.4-mile (57 km) Gotthard Base Tunnel. It will be the longest tunnel in the world when it opens, probably in 2017.

ENGINEERING STRUCTURES AS A SPECTACLE

Railway structures were the wonder of the age from the time of the completion of the stone Causey Arch in County Durham in 1727, the largest single-span bridge in the country until 1756. Travellers came from the Continent to see it, and the impressive structure is now part of a footpath celebrating the area's industrial heritage.

When the Royal Border Bridge at Berwick was nearing completion in 1849, the North British Railway ran an excursion to view 'the stupendous works', and in 1867 the Great Western Railway offered 'The People's Excursion of the Season' to enable the people of Swansea to see Crumlin Viaduct, which had opened 10 years before to become Britain's highest railway viaduct and third highest viaduct in the world. It was scheduled for preservation, but nobody thought to maintain it, so it deteriorated to a point at which demolition was ordered. But not before it had been filmed as part of a scene in the 1966 thriller *Arabesque*, in which Sophia Loren and Gregory Peck rode across the viaduct while being shot at from a helicopter.

OFF THE RAILS

There is a story, possibly apocryphal, of a choir in the Swiss canton of St Gallen which took the train one evening to give a concert on the other side of the 22,225 ft (8,603 m) Ricken Tunnel from their village. They evidently gave one encore too many, for they missed the last train home. There was nothing for it but to walk through the tunnel, knowing that there would be no trains until morning. To keep up their spirits, someone began singing. The acoustics were so good that they decided to pause in their walk and have an impromptu rehearsal. But when they had finished, no one could remember with certainty from which direction they had come ...

INTO THE LAKE

One of the strangest sections of railway ever constructed was a branch into Lake Geneva. It was built in 1963–4 at Monthey to facilitate the launch of Jacques Piccard's *Mesocaphe* submarine, the world's first tourist submarine, which took people beneath the waters of the lake during the 1964 Swiss National Exhibition. Track was built out into the lake for 236 ft (72 m) using floats. These were then removed, allowing the track to sink on to a prepared roadbed. This was consolidated using an old tank locomotive and a wagon of scrap, which were winched up and down until the track was even. This process completely immersed the locomotive and wagon. The 160-tonne, 93 ft 6 in (28.4 m) long submarine was then transported by rail for 10 miles (16 km) from the construction site at Monthey and successfully launched down the slip/railway.

A PRIVATE WORK OF WONDER

One of the most attractive railway viaducts in Cornwall was built by a private landowner to transport minerals, mostly china clay, from his estate to the sea. Joseph Thomas Treffry of Place, near Fowey, developed the harbours at Par and Newquay, and it was to reach the former that he built a horse-drawn tramway which entailed crossing the Luxulyan Valley by a beautifully proportioned 10-arch viaduct, built between 1839 and 1842, 670 ft (204 m) long and 90 ft (27.4 m) high. Besides the standard-gauge tramway, the viaduct carried a leat for 13 waterwheels, including the wheel powering the Carmears inclined plane. The viaduct is a

RAILWAY SIGNS

Sign on Kisumu station, Kenya:

THE FOLLOWING ARTICLES SHALL NOT ALLOWED TO BE KEPT IN THE WAITING ROOM:

1. BUNCHES OF BANANAS
2. CRATES OF FOWLS
3. POTATOES AND CASSAVA
4. HEAVY PACKAGES
5. DIRTY PACKAGES

Scheduled Ancient Monument and part of a World Heritage Site, and the tramway and associated canals can still be followed.

RAILWAY TOWNS

The size of the workshops needed by the larger railway companies often compelled them to choose a site well away from an existing town. Though the amount of land may have been available and cheap, it meant that the railways had to shoulder the burden of creating housing, schools, churches, libraries and recreation facilities for their staff. Towns such as Swindon, Crewe and Horwich were created from small villages, but there were many smaller railway colonies such as Corkerhill near Glasgow, Melton Constable and Woodford Halse.

At Corkerhill the Glasgow & South Western Railway built 132 houses and the Railway Institute, which fulfilled the functions of a church, school, hall, reading-room, library, baths, bank, recreation room and village store. The village of nearly 700 people was self-governing, managed by an annually elected committee of 31 members.

Even a small community such as Oxenholme in Westmorland, junction for Windermere and provider of banking engines for goods trains to Grayrigg, had its football team and children's choir, which helped to raise enough to build the village Mission Hall, where dances and concerts were held.

'CASTLES OF THE NORTH'

This is the name given to the series of railway hotels built across Canada by the railway companies during the late 19th and early 20th centuries, when they were some of the grandest hotels in the world – as they still are. No country bettered Canada in the consistently high standard of its railway hotels. Many were built in the 'château style', a curious blend of Scots baronial and French Renaissance styles that became the signature of a Canadian railway hotel, whichever company built it. The first was Canadian Pacific Railway's Hotel Vancouver, opened in 1888 and the first of three hotels to bear the name in the west coast city. It was followed by CPR's Banff Springs Hotel, Château Frontenac in Quebec City, Place Viger in Montreal – unique in following the British practice of combining hotel with station, The Empress in Victoria and Château Lake Louise in Alberta.

Not every hotel was in this style: The Palliser in Calgary opened in 1914 in an 'Edwardian commercial' style with straight geometric lines that were supposed to suggest the prairie grain elevators found all over the surrounding country. The railway connection has survived the change to Fairmont ownership in the glass rotunda of the Canadian Pacific Pavilion, which showcases CPR history and some of the railway's heritage cars, which can be hired for functions.

Not all have survived: the Winnipeg's CPR Royal Alexandra Hotel of 1906 was demolished in 1971, but astonishingly hundreds of elements of its vast grand café were saved and stored for over 25 years before being re-erected in a 2,800 sq ft (260 sq m) oak-panelled special events room at the Canadian Museum of Rail Travel at Cranbrook, British Columbia.

The largest of the railway hotels is the Royal York in Toronto, opened by the CPR in 1929, when it was the tallest building in the British Empire with 28 floors. It had 1,048 en suite bedrooms, a 12,000-volume library, a concert hall with the finest organ in the country, a

35-operator switchboard and a glassed-in roof garden. Its hand-painted ceilings, travertine pillars and crystal chandeliers still delight guests.

But the CPR's great rival, the Grand Trunk Railway, was determined to match its standards and built the Château Laurier in Ottawa, billed as the country's finest hotel when it opened in 1912. The hotel had been commissioned by the GTR's general manager, Charles Melville, but just 12 days before the hotel's opening he was returning from England with dining-room furniture aboard the *Titanic*. He and all male members of his party went down with the ship. The GTR also built Fort Garry Hotel in Winnipeg, which opened in 1913, and Hotel Macdonald in Edmonton in 1915, before the railway amalgamated with the Canadian National Railway in 1920.

Both CPR and CNR expanded their chains of hotels, ending with the opening in 1958 of the CNR's Queen Elizabeth Hotel in Montreal. The largest hotel in Quebec, it achieved world-wide fame in 1969 when John Lennon and Yoko Ono, having been refused entry to the US, held their bed-in; it was here, in Suite 1742, that Lennon wrote and recorded the song 'Give Peace a Chance'.

In 1988 CPR acquired CNR's hotels and in 1999 changed their name to Fairmont, which continues to operate many of Canada's landmark railway hotels.

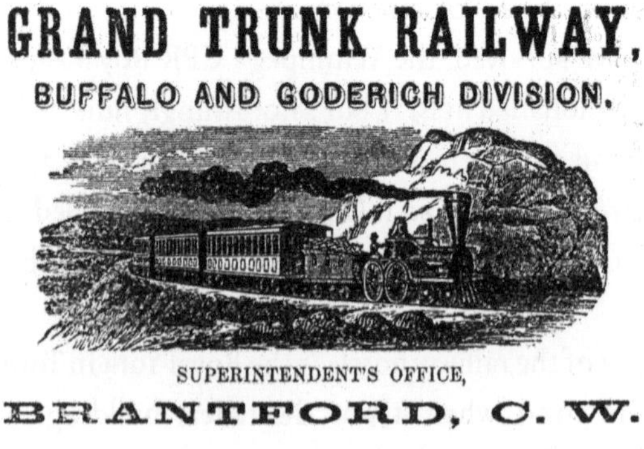

FOR THE RAILWAY THAT NEVER CAME

Several entrepreneurs have been embarrassed by a change in the planned route of a railway, after investing in property to cater for the needs of passengers once the railway was open. One of London's most sumptuous pubs was an example. On Aberdeen Place in St John's Wood stands Grade II-listed Crocker's Folly, sadly boarded up since its closure in 2004. It was built in 1898 as the Crown Hotel by Frank Crocker for passengers arriving at the southern terminus of the last main line built into London, the Great Central Railway. Unfortunately for Crocker, the original location was not thought central enough and it was moved further south to terminate at Marylebone, just north of the Marylebone Road.

Crocker spared no expense in creating a magnificent building with a large marble fireplace, fine tile and glasswork, a grand wooden bar and a richly decorated painted plaster ceiling. It was used for a scene in the film *Georgy Girl*, the 1966 satire on the Swinging Sixties. Given Crocker's grand plans, it is ironic that the pub ended up being closer to the railway's goods depot than to the passenger station and consequently catering for a rather different clientele from the one he anticipated.

A comparable story lies behind a hotel in the Nicola Valley of British Columbia in Canada. The Quilchena Hotel was opened in 1908 by Joseph Guichon, partly in expectation of the railway from Merrit being built through the Nicola Valley to Quilchena, but it never progressed beyond Nicola. It also served the carriage trade on the road from Kamloops to the community of Nicola Lake, then the main settlement in the valley. The hotel closed in 1917 but was reopened by Joseph's grandson in 1958, and the rural building is today one of Canada's most historic hotels.

THE END OF THE BROAD GAUGE

The economics of transport would have been very different had the world adopted as its most common track gauge Brunel's 7 ft rather than Stephenson's 4 ft 8½ in. But the decision to abolish the Great Western Railway's broad gauge was inevitable, given the costs of transhipment and the preponderance of the standard gauge. The operation to convert the last 213 miles (343 km) of broad-gauge track took place over the weekend of 20–23 May 1892 and must rank as the largest engineering possession ever undertaken on Britain's railways. It was meticulously planned.

From the previous Wednesday about 4,200 permanent way men from all parts of the GWR were taken in seven trains to the west, lodging in stations, goods sheds and tents and bringing their own food with them. Straw mattresses and blankets, cooking equipment and oatmeal were provided by the GWR. A gang of 20 men was assigned to roughly a mile (1.6 km) of track, with more at yards and junctions.

The last broad-gauge departure from Paddington was the 10.15am 'Cornishman' on Friday 20 May 1892, witnessed by a large crowd and appropriately hauled by the 'Rover' class *Great Western*. Thousands turned out along the way to witness the end of an era. Conversion work began at daybreak in fine spring weather. Everything that could be done to speed the process had been thought of, even down to making sure every track bolt could be easily turned. On Sunday evening the Night Mail from Paddington took the London & South Western Railway as far as Plymouth, becoming the first train into Cornwall over the converted track, reaching Penzance at 4.40am.

Many were sad to see the end of so distinctive a railway. A dignitary known as the Portreeve of Ashburton (an office dating from 820) enveloped the locomotive hauling the last broad-gauge train from the Devon terminus in black crêpe.

WHAT'S IN A NAME?

On 15 January 1938, Éamon de Valera was travelling from Holyhead to Euston. When it was discovered that the only locomotive available was 'Royal Scot' No. 6122 *Royal Ulster Rifleman*, it was prudently agreed the nameplates should be removed. This proved a wise decision, as his arrival was awaited by a tumultuous reception party which might not have appreciated the irony.

SOUTH-WEST FROM DENVER

The Denver & Rio Grande arguably went through the most spectacular landscapes of any US railroad apart from Alaska. Its most remarkable section of track threaded the Royal Gorge near Canon City, a 10-mile (16 km) long chasm just 50 ft (15 m) across at the bottom and 1,250 ft (380 m) deep in places. Because it is so narrow that no more than a single line could be built through it – and that would be challenge enough – it led to a long conflict between the D&RG and the Santa Fe for the rights to build a line to Leadville and its silver mines. The Royal Gorge War became a two-year struggle, both a physical one between construction gangs and a legal one in courtroom battles that went all the way to the Supreme Court, which ruled in favour of the D&RG in 1879. That was not the end of the affair:

the Santa Fe used every means of undermining the D&RG commercially and physically, leading to further injunctions and even the armed retaking of commandeered locomotives and depots, in which lives were lost. Eventually sense prevailed and the line opened through to Leadville in 1880. It later became part of the main route between Denver and Salt Lake City.

The gorge can still be seen from the trains of the Royal Gorge Route Railroad, which operates a 12-mile (19 km) run from Canon City to Parkdale. One of the highlights is the hanging bridge where the gorge narrows to 30 feet (9 metres) and the railway is suspended over the river by A-frame girders anchored to the rock wall. At this point the canyon walls rise 2,600 feet (792 metres) above the track.

PIEL PIER

Comparable with the sensation of approaching Fleetwood in Lancashire (see page 161) was the railway to the Piel Pier near Barrow at the opposite end of packet sailings from Fleetwood. In 1840 a London banker and MP, John Abel Smith, bought Roa Island at the southern entrance to the Walney Channel. He built a causeway to the mainland and in 1847 opened a pier that projected for 810 ft (247 m) into Walney Channel. The Furness Railway extended the Rampside branch over the causeway to serve the pier from 1846. A storm damaged the pier, but in the 1860s it was rebuilt to allow trains to draw up alongside the boats, which now connected Piel with the Isle of Man and Belfast as well as Fleetwood. After these sailings were lost to Barrow in 1881, Piel Pier decayed and was removed in 1891.

CAPITAL DEVELOPMENT

One of the largest buildings put up by a railway company was the Metropolitan Railway's 11-storey Chiltern Court at London's Baker Street station, designed by Charles Clark. Opened in 1929, it contained offices for the railway, 180 flats (with 30 maids' rooms), 40 passenger and service lifts, and postal chutes on each floor. Residents could access the lower three floors of shops and the restaurant in which John Betjeman was filmed beneath a ceiling of Metropolitan Railway crests in the making of the classic 1973 documentary *Metro-land.* It is now a Wetherspoon's pub. Chiltern Court was the capital's most luxurious apartment block when it opened, and early residents included the novelists H.G. Wells (at No. 47) and Arnold Bennett.

WATKIN'S FOLLY

Sir Edward Watkin (1819–1901) was one of the most prominent railway managers and chairmen in Britain in the late 19th century. He was chairman of three major companies and a driving force in efforts to build a Channel Tunnel. A venture associated with the Metropolitan Railway, one of his chairmanships, was the Metropolitan Tower Co., which bought 280 acres (113 ha) of land at Wembley Park. The centrepiece of the development was to be a tower that would eclipse even the Eiffel Tower. Watkin invited Eiffel to design the tower, but he declined, replying that if he undertook the commission, the French people 'would not think me so good a Frenchman as I hope I am'. Legs of 300 ft (91 m) were to support a superstructure 700 ft (213 m) high, but it never progressed beyond the first landing, which opened in 1896. The surrounding amusement park was finished and became a popular attraction before the site was redeveloped for the British Empire Exhibition of 1924–5. The tower was demolished in 1907.

AN ELECTRIC RABBIT WARREN

A short-lived private company experiment was made in London in the 1870s to move mail around the capital by underground tunnel; it used a larger version of the kind of pneumatic tubes once found shuttling change and receipts around big department stores, but it was evidently not a success.

To overcome the chronic traffic congestion of London's streets, the idea was revived, and in 1908 a team of Post Office engineers visited the Chicago freight subway system and a similar system in Berlin, Germany. The Post Office Railway was authorised in 1913, and the 6½-mile (10.5 km) main tunnel was built in time to act as a storage facility for objects from the Tate Gallery, the National Portrait Gallery, the British Museum and the Wallace Collection during the First World War. The 2 ft gauge line finally opened for Christmas parcels in 1927 and for letters the following February, linking Paddington with the Whitechapel Eastern Delivery Office via seven intermediate stops.

The driverless trains operated under the streets of London until 2003. The railway is now officially mothballed, but no visits are allowed. The only alternative is to watch the 1991 action comedy *Hudson Hawk*, starring Bruce Willis, in which the railway assumes the role of a private system underneath the Vatican. Chicago's system, in contrast, was adapted to carry the city's rubbish.

'THAT NOBLE ARCH OF BARON MUNCHAUSEN'

This was the phrase used by the *Railway Times* to pour scorn on the idea of bridging the Solway Firth at the west end of Hadrian's Wall. Some in the 1860s considered it impossible to bridge an estuary notorious for shifting sands and treacherous tides. But the Solway Junction Railway succeeded in constructing a 5,820 ft (1,774 m) bridge, linking Bowness with Seafield, using 193 cast-iron columns protected against the tides by timber buttresses. The Solway Viaduct opened to mineral traffic in 1869 and to passengers the following year. Then the longest viaduct in Britain, it carried only a single track, though a short section of 12 piers was built as a guide for a second track should demand require it. With a healthy cross-border traffic of northbound haematite from Cumberland to the Lanarkshire steel mills, it seemed the doubters had been put in their place.

The viaduct was always subject to a 10 mph (16 kph) speed restriction, but serious trouble came during the winter of 1875–6 when ice formed in the piers and produced cracks. Worse followed in 1881 with the destruction of 45 piers by ice floes. Moreover the Cumberland ores were almost worked out, and the line was closed during the First World War. It reopened in 1920, but years of minimal maintenance had taken their toll and traffic was too meagre to justify the high cost of full repair. The viaduct was condemned in August 1921 but remained for over a decade as a rare instance of a closed railway, looking forlorn and almost eerie in photographs of the time. It was used by brave pedestrians, especially by Scots in search of a drink on Sunday nights when their own hostelries were closed. Demolition began in 1934 and took 18 months.

SYMBOL OF A RAILWAY

Ribblehead Viaduct is one of the most dramatically situated structures on a British railway. It came to prominence during the long campaign to save the Settle & Carlisle railway, finally reprieved in 1989 by Michael Portillo, who regards this as his greatest achievement. It became the focus of the campaign because British Rail used a repair figure for the viaduct of £4.5–6 million as justification for shutting the line. Opponents questioned the sum and were vindicated when repairs were completed in 1992 for £3 million.

Despite its wild setting, the viaduct must be one of the most photographed viaducts in the country, its 24 arches striding gracefully across the moorland. Every sixth pier was 18 ft (5.5 m) thick instead of 6 ft (1.8 m) thick in anticipation of the effect of wind with which railwaymen soon became familiar. The ferocity was sometimes so great that they had to cross the viaduct on hands and knees in the lee of the parapet. In steam days firemen would build up the fire before the viaduct, because the wind could blow coal off the shovel. On 8 December 1965 seven new cars from Luton were blown off a northbound train. In an extraordinary incident, a track ganger had his cap blown off; it sailed under an arch and landed back on his head the wrong way round – but, as he said, 'Thou can't have ivverything.'

A TUNNEL BONUS

Working as a platelayer in tunnels during steam days was not the most pleasant of occupations. Tunnels on busy, steeply graded lines where ascending locomotives were working hard might seldom clear of smoke on still days, while badly loaded tenders might shed lumps of coal. Recesses in the tunnel walls provided a very necessary refuge. On the Settle & Carlisle in the 1930s the gangers responsible for tunnels such as Rise Hill and Blea Moor received an extra 2s 6d (12½p) a week and a soap ration.

SPANNING THE ZAMBESI

It was Cecil Rhodes's wish that the Cape-to-Cairo railway should cross the Zambesi close enough to the Victoria Falls for passengers to feel the spray. He was humoured in this fancy by his close friend Sir Charles Metcalfe, even though there would have been a much easier crossing 6 miles (9.6 km) up river beyond Kandahar Island. The result is one of the world's great bridges, a single delicate span of steel providing a spectacular view of the falls and the gorge, but Rhodes never lived to see it, dying in 1902.

The contract for construction was given to the Cleveland Bridge & Engineering Co. of Darlington and began about October 1903 with the firing of a rocket to take a fine string across the chasm. It succeeded on the third attempt. Progressively thicker and heavier cables were pulled across to allow first a bosun's chair and then a Blondin overhead carrier to transport up to 15 tons at a time across the river. The graceful arch has a span of 500 ft (152 m), and its prefabricated steelwork was shipped to Beira. The opening ceremony took place on 12 September 1905, carried out by Professor George Darwin, son of Charles Darwin, who was in Rhodesia leading a party of scientists on behalf of the British Association.

THE WORLD'S FLATTEST ARCH

When I.K. Brunel took on the task of designing a bridge to carry the Great Western Railway across the Thames at Maidenhead, the Thames Commissioners set him a challenge by stipulating that it must not obstruct the broad navigation channel or the towpath beside it. This meant using only a single pier on a small island, and since the height of the railway on the approaches was no greater than the mast of a sailing barge, Brunel was forced to design arches so flat that his detractors thought they were bound to fail. The arches rose just 28 ft (8.5 m) for a span of 128 ft (39 m). Imagine their delight when one of the arches did distort by half an inch when the centrings were eased without Brunel's blessing. And their dismay when the contractor, to his credit, admitted he was at fault in moving the centrings before the Roman cement had fully set. The GWR directors gave instructions for the centrings to remain through the winter, but in fact Brunel had already eased them. It has been suggested that Brunel was toying with the sceptics. A gale blew down the wooden framework and the bridge stood, as it has to the present, carrying trains at twice the speed Brunel could have envisaged. It remains the flattest arch in Britain, if not the world, and was chosen by Turner as the subject of *Rain, Steam and Speed.*

CHAPTER THREE

THE RAILWAY STATION

FOR OVER A century the railway station was the focal point of life in every city, town and village served by one. The stationmaster was a figure on a par with the bank manager in the days when both were respected pillars of the community. Commercial life revolved around the railway with the carriage of almost all goods, parcels and mail. The buildings varied tremendously, from an apology barely distinguishable from a garden shed to some of the finest civic buildings. Even little communities on more prosperous railways enjoyed impressive buildings, such as Brunel's smaller Italianate stations on the Great Western, G.T. Andrews's designs for the North Eastern Railway or the large stone stations between Alnwick and Coldstream in the sparsely populated country on the border of England and Scotland. Stations acted as magnets for children, not only for the perennial appeal of a steam train passing, but for the coming and going of people, the constant activity of a goods yard, and the sound of bell codes emanating from the signal-box.

IMPROVING THE CIVIC REALM

The early railway companies built stations to reassure the public of the solidity and dependability of railways and railway travel. The great Doric Arch at Euston and its Ionic counterpart at Curzon Street station in Birmingham were meant to impress. Some cities quickly saw the potential for such buildings to aggrandise their centres: in 1836 the Common Council of Liverpool made a contribution of £2,000 towards 'beautification' of Lime Street station (not today's building but its predecessor), and around the same time Rugby School gave £1,000 for the railway to be borne across the road by a Gothic arch.

FROM ANOTHER AGE

Not all cities had stations their status deserved. When Matthew Arnold said that Oxford University was 'whispering the last enchantments of the Middle Ages', Max Beerbohm thought he must have been referring to the railway station (the original building).

The grand cathedrals of the steam age still contribute a sense of occasion to a railway journey. So unsuccessful and rebarbative were the successors built in the architecturally dark days of the 1960s and '70s that both Birmingham New Street and London Euston are being rebuilt.

MAKING DO

Not every railway company could afford a fine station building – or one at all in some cases. The prize for improvisation could have been awarded to the Shrewsbury & Hereford Railway for its first 'station' at Moreton-on-Lugg, which made use of the hollow trunk of a venerable tree. There was no station at the Somerset village of Farrington Gurney, but the Great Western Railway provided a ticket office in a tiny extension to the Miner's Arms public house where tickets could be bought until 7pm by ringing the bell; the nearest station was Hallatrow, 1¼ miles (2 km) away. The Midland Railway could certainly afford decent buildings, but it never got round to replacing the station at Damens on the previously independent Keighley & Worth Valley Railway (now a heritage railway); this was so small that a farmer is supposed to have taken it away, thinking it was the hen house he had ordered. The halt at Dilton Marsh between Westbury and Warminster in Wiltshire had no booking office, but for decades from 1947 Mrs H. Roberts sold tickets on a commission basis, a large sign on the station requesting passengers to 'please obtain tickets from Mrs H. Roberts, "Holmdale", 7th house up the hill'. Fierce protests against planned closure succeeded in saving the station, and John Betjeman commemorated the halt in a poem:

Dilton Marsh Halt

Was it worth keeping the Halt open,
We thought as we looked at the sky
Red through the spread of the cedar-tree,
With the evening train gone by?

Yes, we said, for in summer the anglers use it,
Two and sometimes three
Will bring their catches of rods and poles and perches
To Westbury, home for tea.

There isn't a porter. The platform is made of sleepers.
The guard of the last train puts out the light
And high over lorries and cattle the Halt unwinking
Waits through the Wiltshire night.

O housewife safe in the comprehensive churning
Of the Warminster launderette!
O husband down at the depot with car in car-park!
The Halt is waiting yet.

And when all the horrible roads are finally done for,
And there's no more petrol left in the world to burn,
Here to the Halt from Salisbury and from Bristol
Steam trains will return.

A MIGHTY BEER CELLAR

The transformation of St Pancras as the terminal for Eurostar is largely thanks to the Victorian capital's desire for Burton beer. The undercroft of the station, where people now shop and await their departure for Paris or Brussels, is supported by 720 columns and was designed by W.H. Barlow to accommodate as many barrels of beer as possible. After the station was opened in 1868, beer traffic was handled in the centre of the station between platforms 4 and 5. A central third track ended in a wagon hoist which lowered wagons 20 ft (6 m) below rail level. Beer storage ended in 1967.

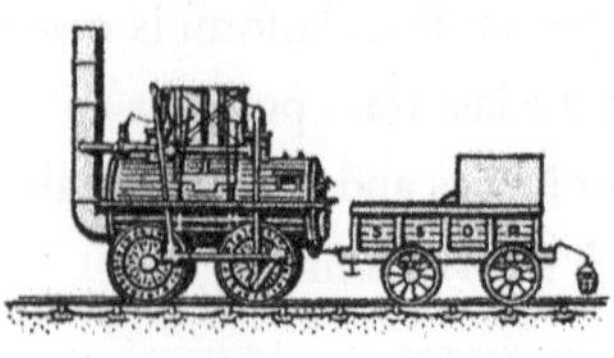

SUFFRAGETTE ASSAULTS

The campaign to obtain votes for women gathered momentum from 1869, but only began to affect the railways in 1912, with various acts of vandalism. In one of them, a wealthy young man who was a member of the Men's Political Union for Women's Enfranchisement set fire to a first-class compartment in a Great Central Railway carriage at Harrow. In court he said he didn't recognise 'men-made laws'. At Potters Bar a saboteur used sash cord to render a signal inoperative, and left a note: 'The only way to stop this trouble is to remove the cause by giving votes to women.'

Two stations were the target of militant suffragettes in March 1913. The station at Croxley Green had only been open since the previous June, as the terminus of a 1¼-mile (2 km) branch line, when Croxley's policeman directed a group of ladies to the station and bid them 'Good night'. The blaze that followed was so fierce that firemen were able to save only the booking office, which was at a lower level than the other station buildings. A few days later the perpetrators thoughtfully sent a copy of a Suffragette newspaper to the Croxley stationmaster with a note reading 'Afraid copy left got burnt'. Saunderton station in Buckinghamshire was also comparatively new, having been built in 1901, and here the booking office was burnt out. Placards reading 'Votes for Women' and 'Burning to get the Vote' were left on the platform.

The worst attack was at Leuchars Junction in Fife on 30 June 1913, when the station was almost completely destroyed by fire, but the North Eastern Railway also lost its station at Kenton, on the branch to Ponteland in Northumberland, on 13 September. Here a note suggested: 'Asquith is responsible for militancy. Apply to him for the damage.'

Crude home-made incendiary devices and bombs were also used, fortunately without loss of life. One of the two men who in April 1913 attempted to blow up the gents toilet at Oxted in Surrey was eventually revealed to be Harold Laski, later Professor of Political Philosophy at London School of Economics and chairman of the Labour Party in 1945–6. After the incident he escaped to Dover and hid in Paris for a few weeks, eluding identification and arrest. Bombs left at Aberdeen station and London's Liverpool Street station failed to explode, and a ticking bomb found at Aylesbury station was dumped in a bucket of water by a porter.

The affluent background of the few people who carried out these largely night-time attacks is attested by their use of a car, then the preserve of the well-to-do.

WORSHIP AT STATIONS

It was quite common for Bibles to be found in railway waiting rooms, like Gideon Bibles in hotel bedrooms. During a visit in 1862 the French historian Hippolyte Taine was astonished to find chained Bibles for travellers to read at London railway stations. In the 1870s a director of the Taff Vale Railway left £100 in his will for books of Psalms and the New Testament to be provided in the company's waiting rooms. Bible classes were held on Sunday afternoons in the second-class ladies' waiting room at Portsmouth Town station.

THE LAST JOURNEY

The growth of cities in the 19th century put pressure on space in cemeteries. To overcome this, mortuary companies created out-of-town cemeteries that could be reached by train. Waterloo had a private station designed by Sir William Tite for funeral trains to depart for the 2,000-acre (809 ha) cemetery in the Surrey countryside at Brockwood, opened in 1854 and reached by way of Necropolis Junction and a ¾-mile (1.2 km) branch line. The station had mortuary slabs and coffin lifts. Three classes of coffin fares (single only), were available to maintain class distinctions.

THE READING PUBLIC

W.H. Smith's first railway bookstall opened on 1 November 1848 at Euston station, following a tender submitted to the London & North Western Railway for sole bookstall rights on its stations. A similar deal was signed with the Midland Railway a fortnight later, and contracts with other railway companies followed. In 1851 W.H. Smith won the first contract to handle advertising rights at stations, again with the LNWR.

REMOTE REFRESHMENTS

Perhaps the most remote station buffet in Britain was Riccarton Junction, a wind-blasted junction on the Waverley route between Carlisle and

Edinburgh. A sheet of frosted glass in the single-storey station advertised a 'Tea Room' where a lady – probably the stationmaster's wife – served pots of tea and hot scones. The station was so isolated that there was no road to it, so the branch of the Hawick Co-operative Society in the station was vital for the small railway community.

THE FRUIT STALL MENACE

The compensation culture is spoken of as a modern phenomenon, but a passenger in 1911 sued the Metropolitan Railway after slipping on a banana skin at the foot of the stairs leading to a platform. Though the railway produced evidence that the premises were swept twice a day, the jury found in the passenger's favour and awarded compensation of £500; in 1913 average annual earnings were £51. Contemporary coverage envisaged the wholesale removal of fruit stalls from stations and suggested firework stalls would be less risky.

FOUR-LEGGED FRIENDS

Tim, an Irish Terrier, was owned by an inspector on the Great Western Railway, John Bush, and collected £795 at Paddington station from May 1892, including two sovereigns, one placed in his box by command of Queen Victoria upon her arrival at Paddington on 8 March 1900. When Tim died, he was stuffed and then stood in a case on Paddington station until the 1950s.

THE PERILS OF STATION LIFE IN KENYA

Construction of the Uganda Railway from Mombasa to Nairobi was plagued by nocturnal attacks from man-eating lions on the construction camp at Tsavo River. *The Man-Eaters of Tsavo* by the engineer in charge, ex-Sergeant J.H. Patterson, tells the story of his eventual success in overcoming them. But memory of another such episode has survived better, thanks to a carriage in Nairobi Railway Museum which provided the setting for this gruesome incident.

Operations on the Uganda Railway were also blighted by attacks on railway workers from lions with a taste for humans, and several members of staff were lost at the station of Kima. One night the lion responsible clambered on to the station roof and tried to tear off the corrugated-iron sheets to find his dinner, which prompted perhaps the strangest railway telegram: 'Lion fighting with station. Send urgent succour.'

An engine driver volunteered to sit up one night in an iron water tank after having a loop cut in the side through which to fire. It must have been on a flimsy structure, because the lion toppled it over before the driver could fire a shot. The terrified man managed to crouch low in the tank, which was too narrow for the lion to squeeze into, but was unable to take proper aim and his shot only scared the lion away.

On 6 June 1900 Captain Charles Henry Ryall, superintendent of the Uganda Railway Police, was travelling from Makindu to Nairobi in his inspection saloon with two traders named Parenti and Huebner. When they arrived at Kima, they heard that the lion had been seen only hours before, so Ryall had his saloon placed in a siding near the station. Construction works were still unfinished, and the siding was not perfectly level, giving the carriage a list. That night they hoped to attract the lion and have the opportunity to dispatch him. Ryall was on first watch but must have gone to sleep on his berth. The lion entered the carriage from the end balcony through an unlocked sliding door, but the tilt and the weight of the lion caused the door to slide shut after the lion had entered the carriage.

Parenti was sleeping on the floor, and the lion had to stand on him as he chose to seize Ryall. The only escape for Huebner in the upper berth was to go through a sliding door into the servants' quarters, opposite the door by which the lion had entered. In the confines of the carriage Huebner had to jump on to the lion's back to reach the interior door, and the lion was so engaged with Ryall that he ignored the movement. But the servants were holding the door shut, and only by an adrenalin-charged effort could Huebner prise it open to reach safety. Poor Ryall was dragged out through the window and into the bush. Parenti clambered out of another window and ran to the station building to send a telegram to Kiu for help.

Ryall's body was found and taken to Nairobi for burial in the European cemetery, where his grave has been recently restored. His mother offered £100 for the lion's pelt, but it eluded a small army of hunters for over three months. Finally it was trapped in a cage and shot, ending the depredations at Kima. The carriage was preserved and for many years stood on a platform at Nairobi station before being moved to the museum.

OUTPOSTS OF THE RAILWAY EMPIRE

The railways created some exceptionally remote communities, sometimes of just a few families. The need for long sections of single line to be broken up by passing places, or double-track lines to have a 'block post' to increase line capacity, compelled railways in the days of mechanical signalling to build some very remote signal-boxes. The men looking after the track also had to live beside the section of line for which they were responsible. Most of Britain's loneliest outposts were to be found in Scotland. At these places, the sense of isolation was acute and was captured by Charles Dickens in his 1866 short story 'The Signalman'.

The railway which until 1965 carried express boat trains to Stranraer from Carlisle had such a place at Loch Skerrow, between Gatehouse of Fleet and New Galloway. The signal-box was open continuously except for a short period on Sundays, requiring three signalmen to live near the wooden signal-box and watering point for steam locomotives. The Highland main line between Perth and Inverness had two particularly isolated crossing places: Inchlea cabin (as the Highland Railway called signal-boxes) was in such an exposed position that it had an inside staircase; Slochd had two cabins because it was the summit of a climb from both directions and assisting locomotives were detached here.

Two of the most remote railway postings in Britain were Corrour and Gorton, where passing loops on the single line between Glasgow and Fort William allowed trains to cross. Corrour appeared in public timetables from 1934, but the railway was most reluctant to allow any access to Gorton. A Glasgow journalist wanting to write a feature on the community was refused access, and when someone succeeded in writing about it, local railway staff received 'please explain' letters from higher authority.

For many years the two shifts at Gorton were covered by a signalman and his daughter. There was no public station there, but the early morning train stopped specially to pick up the children of railway workers living in the few cottages to take them to school at Rannoch, a timetabled station though a desolate spot in the middle of the moor made famous by Robert Louis Stevenson in *Kidnapped*. Children living in lineside cottages further north were picked up by a morning train and taken to school in Fort William. After Easter 1938, however, the school at Rannoch became overcrowded, and so the railway company set up a school at Gorton in an old railway carriage on the platform, and Argyll County Council provided a teacher from Bridge of Orchy to instruct the pupils, who once reached 11 in number.

Saplings were planted around the moorland cottages to act as windbreaks, and clumps of trees became railway landmarks in the desolate landscape. The water on Rannoch is unsafe, so the first train of the day stopped to deliver 12 buckets of water from the locomotive tender to the cottages. After dieselisation it was brought from Fort William in more hygienic containers. If emergency medical help were needed, a locomotive would take a doctor from Fort William or Tulloch. This was an unenviable assignment, because it meant running tender-first for many miles on the return journey, there being no means of turning a locomotive. Tender-first running on the West Highland was avoided at all costs, and on one occasion the three men were so chilled that the fireman could hardly hold the shovel.

When railwaymen from these places went on holiday, a rather particular breed of relief man was required: a portable bed, cooking apparatus, fishing rod and a snare wire were necessary accoutrements. Sometimes the same train delivering the relief man picked up the family he was replacing, so there was time for only a brief exchange. One man found a note for him in the kitchen detailing not railway matters but instructions on how to look after the poultry, cats, dog and three goats.

Isolated railway communities had to be self-reliant. At the lonely junction of Hawes (now named Garsdale) on the Settle & Carlisle, church services were held in the waiting room on the northbound platform, accompanied by a small harmonium, while the ladies' waiting room contained the library. This was generously supplied with 150 books in about 1900 by two elderly ladies who had taken pity on this isolated community. The 'community hall' occupied the stone base of the water tank for locomotives, and here whist drives, suppers, concerts and dances were held, with music supplied by a piano or gramophone.

Probably the remotest railway community in the world is Cook, on the dead-straight 297-mile (478 km) section of track across South Australia's desolate Nullarbor Plain. It was once a community of 40, and until 1996 it had a weekly Tea and Sugar train delivering provisions, but in 2009 it had shrunk to just 2.

SHARPSHOOTING STATIONMASTER

During the First World War, the campaign in East Africa was fought by guerilla actions and much smaller forces than those in the European theatre. The railway line between Nairobi and the coast at Mombasa was the subject of raids by troops under General Paul Emil von Lettow-Vorbeck, and on one occasion a lonely stationmaster tapped out a message to Nairobi: 'One hundred German soldiers approaching station, please send on next train one rifle and one hundred bullets.'

AN EQUITABLE REFUND AT SWINDON

In the days before dining-cars, when trains stopped at stations for passengers to bolt some indifferent fare, a foreigner who patronised the refreshment room at Swindon had some soup and was then handed someone else's change. When he rejoined the train, he extolled to his fellow passengers the arrangement by which a passenger was entitled to a refund if he didn't consume the whole dish.

THE BUSIEST SIGNAL-BOXES

A large signal-box in the days of mechanical signalling required mental agility and a certain amount of physical strength; long stretches of point rodding and distant signals could demand hefty pulls. On more than one occasion a signalman, accustomed to the amount of effort required by a particular lever, went backwards through a window when he forgot that motor-assistance had been installed.

Movements at Glasgow Central before the First World War were controlled by a single large cabin on the bridge across the Clyde. With 371 levers, it was normally worked by three men and two boys, one logging times and the other attending to the many telephones. The concentration required was reflected in an eight-hour shift, though this was one of the few boxes at the time that required minimal force, since signals and points were electro-pneumatic, using motors operated by compressed air.

TEMPLES OF CONVENIENCE

Railway station lavatories were not noted for the luxury of their appointments, but the toilet off the oak-panelled first-class waiting room at the Great Northern and London & North Western joint station at Melton Mowbray in Leicestershire had a hot-water pipe coursing through the seat.

GREAT NORTHERN RAILWAY

ATTRACTING EDWARDIAN GUESTS

The 1906 Great Western Railway holiday guide to Devon, which ran to 266 pages, employed the period's typically idiosyncratic use of capital letters in its adverts: 'The Hotel is under the Personal Supervision of the Proprietor and his Wife, and is specially adapted for Families & Tourists, and ELECTRIC LIGHT throughout.' Another boasted that it was 'at one time occupied by the late Grand Duke Sergius [Tsar Alexander III's brother, who had been killed by a bomb in Moscow the previous year] and other members of the Russian Royal Family'. More prosaically, another listed its speciality as 'Eclipse Special Pale Ales and Invalid Stout in bottle'.

FACILITIES AT EUSTON

When London's current unloved station at Euston was opened in 1968, complaints were made about the lack of so basic an amenity as seats for waiting passengers; they were deliberately omitted in case people not using trains should sit on them. Contrast this with the facilities provided in 1911. There was a Writing Room off the great hall, with paper and pens as well as stenographers to whom letters could be dictated and who would then type them 'while you wait'. Foreigners could request an

RAILWAY SIGNS

A notice on the platform of Ingra Tor Halt on Dartmoor warned: 'In the interests of Game Preservation and for their protection against the bites of snakes etc., dogs should be kept on a lead.' One wonders what was covered by the 'etc.'.

interpreter from the Enquiry Office, and District Messengers would be dispatched to anywhere within the metropolis. There was a suite of Hairdressing and Toilet Saloons, with bathrooms and dressing rooms. Kennels and stables were available. For journeys Luncheon and Tea Baskets were provided for journeys (despite the generous provision of restaurant cars).

The Ladies' Waiting Room was carpeted, and vases of flowers were placed on tables between the easy chairs. The adjacent dressing room had a porcelain bath and dressing table with brushes, combs, hat pins, hair curlers and an electric apparatus for heating them.

PRIVATE ROYAL STATIONS

Today Queen Elizabeth II sometimes takes a service train to King's Lynn for Sandringham. Queen Victoria would not have been amused at the suggestion. For her visits to Osborne House on the Isle of Wight, the London & South Western Railway even extended its Gosport branch to terminate at Clarence Yard private station. From the 560 ft (171 m) platform with long umbrella roof extending over the single track, a covered bay led to the embarkation pontoon where she would board her steamer.

WAITING FOR INSPIRATION

The idea that Paul Simon wrote 'Homeward Bound' while waiting for a train at Widnes in 1965 would seem to be a myth. He stayed with a Widnes family while on the tour, but he only just caught the train back to his then home at Brentwood in Essex, so had no time either to write lyrics or try some chords. During an interview with *SongTalk* magazine in 1990, Paul Simon stated that it was written in Liverpool during the same tour.

TAKE THE 'A' TRAIN

The suburban services on the lines to Enfield, Chingford and Palace Gates from London's Liverpool Street station became so busy that carriages were given distinctive yellow and blue stripes to denote first and second class respectively, earning them the soubriquet of Jazz Trains. The colours were intended to help passengers find their compartment more quickly. A later manager, the redoubtable Gerard Fiennes, had martial music played over the loudspeakers between train announcements to encourage swifter movement of the crowds.

CHARING CROSS ROOF COLLAPSE

Structural failure on the railways has been rare, thanks to the early builders constructing bridges and viaducts capable of taking much heavier weights than the trains of their day. The only major example of failure among the great roofs covering main stations occurred on 5 December 1905 when a 100-ton iron girder supporting the roof over Charing Cross station crashed on to unoccupied carriages below. One of the 30 men scraping and painting the great arched roof was carried to his death, and worse was to follow. Mercifully the station was promptly evacuated, for within minutes 70 ft (21 m) of roof, comprising two bays, collapsed, killing two more workmen who had not been able to reach safety in time. The outer wall on the west side of the station bowed outwards and crashed into the Avenue Theatre (now the Playhouse Theatre) which was under reconstruction and full of workmen, three of whom were killed. The cause of the disaster was never fully understood, only that it had begun with the failure of a tie-rod.

ESSEX DEBUT

Blur (when they were called Seymour) played their first gig in the late 1980s in the goods shed at Chappel & Wakes Colne station near Colchester, now part of the East Anglian Railway Museum. The band celebrated its reunion by having a concert there in June 2009, mainly for family and friends with a few tickets for sale to raise money for the museum and Aldham Village Hall. A plaque erected by the Performing Rights Society on the goods shed commemorates the events.

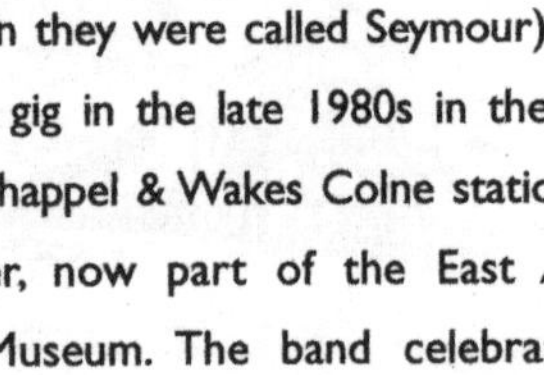

FIRST RAILWAY ESCALATOR

The first UK use of a moving inclined platform without steps was at Harrods of Knightsbridge in 1898, but its first railway application three years later was at Seaforth Sands station on the Liverpool Overhead Railway, colloquially known as the 'dockers' umbrella'. The stepless escalator lasted only until 1906, when it was removed because of all the demands for compensation from ladies when the long skirts of the day were caught in the apparatus.

The first 'moving stairway' on the London Underground was installed in 1911 at Earls Court, linking the underground Great Northern, Piccadilly & Brompton Railway (now the Piccadilly Line) with the Metropolitan District Railway (District Line). It was the first example located in a tubular tunnel and could carry 10,800 people an hour in each direction.

'BUMPER' HARRIS

To allay public anxiety about use of the first escalator on the Underground, a one-legged man named William 'Bumper' Harris demonstrated how easy it was. Cynics suggested they knew how he had lost his other leg, but newspapers reported people breaking their journey to experience this novelty. The idea that Harris was paid to ride up and down it all day is untrue: Harris was employed by Mowlem & Cochrane as Clerk of Works on Underground projects. He retired to Oldend Hall in Stonehouse,

Gloucestershire, where he made cider. Six walking sticks were made out of prehistoric oak found during the excavations at Earls Court; one was given to Harris and is on loan from his family to the London Transport Museum. It can be viewed on the museum's website.

UNSCRAMBLING THE UNDERGROUND

The most famous railway map in the world nearly didn't see the light of day. When Harry Beck (1903–74), a draughtsman in the signalling department, first showed his idea to the publicity committee in 1931, it was rejected. He tried again the following year and, after successful trials, 750,000 copies were printed for free distribution. The genius of the map is to discard geography in the interest of clarity, and the formula was adopted by other cities, including New York, Sydney and Berlin, and even national railways. It is thought that Beck was paid just five guineas for the original concept, yet London Underground has made millions of pounds through licensing the design. His only other recognition is a plaque at Finchley Central, the station nearest his home.

STAND ON THE RIGHT

In most countries, it is customary for passengers using metro escalators to follow the rules of the road – drive on the right, stand on the right. But not on the London Underground. For many years, standing on the right was thought to have been an arbitrary decision, but restoration of a film in 2009 suggests a logical reason. The steps of modern 'comb' escalators are at right angles to the direction of travel, but the first escalators used on the Underground were of the 'shunt' type on a diagonal that ended for the right foot first. This forced passengers to step off using the right foot first, which was considered the safer way. For descending passengers, those walking down and by definition in a hurry had an extra section of escalator by using the left-hand side. The last 'shunt' escalator was taken out in 1953, from Liverpool Street, while the first of the 'comb' type was installed at Clapham Common in 1924.

The 1928 film *Underground*, directed by Anthony Asquith, son of Prime Minister Herbert Asquith, extracted comedy from the convention by showing a confused soldier, accustomed to always starting to march with the left foot, stumbling at the end of the escalator. Asquith was best known for *The Browning Version* (1951) and *Carrington VC* (1954).

TYPEFACE FOR A CAPITAL

The typography of the London Underground and the appearance of the distinctive blue and red station signs were the work of Edward Johnston (1872–1944), who was commissioned by the remarkable Frank Pick to design a new typeface. The sans-serif face was used throughout the London Underground until the 1980s when it was gently updated. Johnston is regarded as one of the fathers of modern calligraphy and taught Eric Gill. Born in Uruguay, he lived in Hammersmith until 1912, when he followed his former pupil Gill to Ditchling in Sussex. It was there that he worked on the typeface now known as New Johnston and used by Transport for London.

CAROL SERVICES

A carol service used to be held in the magnificent Greek-idiom Great Hall at old Euston station, designed by Philip Charles Hardwick. A huge Christmas tree filled the 64 ft (19.5 m) high hall, which measured 128 ft (39 m) by 62 ft (19 m), and a choir stood on the staircase leading up to a colonnade of Ionic columns.

DOOR TO DOOR

The railway-built Zetland Hotel at the terminus station of Saltburn on the Yorkshire coast had an entrance directly off the end of the platform, with a separate overall roof to protect guests. Designed by William Peachey, the hotel was also remarkable for the semicircular tower room in the centre of its seafront façade, which was used as a telescope room. Edward VII when Prince of Wales was a regular guest.

A different door-to-door service was provided at the London Midland & Scottish Railway's Welcombe Hotel near Stratford-on-Avon. A 'Ro-Railer' convertible bus ran from Blisworth station, connecting with trains from Euston. After running on rails to a special ramp in Stratford goods yard, the bus lowered its rubber-tyred wheels and retracted its rail wheels before taking to tarmac to reach the hotel.

STATION BELLS

It was once common practice for the passage of a train to be presaged by the ringing of a handbell or gong, the automated versions causing an unnecessary stir among waiting passengers as a goods train trundled through. An unusual example was mounted on a wall bracket at Lossiemouth station in Morayshire. The large bell was engraved 'Lady Gordon 1785' and had been taken from her dower house at Lossiemouth House by a sea captain who bought the house after her death. He had it set up at the harbour as a warning of ship arrivals and departures. After the arrival of the railway in 1852 put paid to passenger ship services, it was taken to the station and rung five minutes before and at departure time as a service to watchless fishwives and drinkers at the station hotel. It was still in use in 1963. The line closed to passengers in 1964, but the bell is apparently safe in someone's garage in the town.

GILDED COMFORT

Landowners often imposed conditions on the railway in return for an agreement to sell land. One of the most common was provision of a private station or waiting room. The former included two in Cumberland: Dovenby for the Ballantine Dykes family and Crofton for Sir Musgrave Brisco, Bt. In Wiltshire the Marquess of Lansdowne had a semi-private station at Black Dog on the branch from Chippenham to Calne. He was happy for others to use it, but it was not to appear in the public timetable; it emerged from anonymity only in 1952. It had two private sidings, one for loading racehorses and another for transferring silverware between country estate and London residence. Lord Lansdowne agreed to supply a rent-free house and free fuel for the stationmaster, as well as 50 per cent of his wages. The railway, in turn, agreed not to appoint anyone without the Marquess's consent, which entailed an interview. The Duke of Rutland had a special apartment in Redmile & Belvoir station with a coat of arms above the entrance, while the Earl of Harrowby merited a covered cab entrance reached through an avenue of chestnuts at Sandon in Staffordshire.

It was not only aristocrats who could create separate station facilities. The famous singer Adelina Patti had a private waiting room with silver taps in its lavatory at Craig-y-Nos station on the Neath & Brecon Railway. Since 1878 she had owned the nearby castle of the same name, and many illustrious guests arrived by train, including Prince Henry of Battenberg, the Crown Prince of Sweden and, it is thought, Edward VII.

Some landowners could also request a special stop. The Midland Railway would accept a request from Sir Julius Wernher of Luton Hoo in Bedfordshire for a train to stop for him at Chiltern Green station between Harpenden and Luton.

OFF THE RAILS

In 1846 the huge Barentin Viaduct between Paris and Rouen being built by the English contractor Thomas Brassey collapsed as the track was being ballasted. Without any argument over the liability, Brassey said he would rebuild it at his own cost: 'I have contracted to make and maintain the road [railway], and nothing shall prevent Thomas Brassey from being as good as his word.' It cost him £40,000. By the time he died at 65 in 1870, he had built one-twentieth of the world's railways in his own name – there was never a Brassey company to limit his liability.

BLINDED BY SMOKE

Unlike their counterparts on exposed moorland lines, a few unfortunate signalmen were not just oblivious to the weather but deprived of daylight, whatever time their shift. Beneath London's St Pancras station a tunnel was built to link the Midland Railway at St Paul's Junction with the Metropolitan 'Widened Lines'; it now carries Thameslink services. In its depths was a small gas-lit signal cabin known as St Pancras Tunnel Box. Behind a locked door off the cab ramp on the west side of the station, a narrow spiral staircase descended to the Stygian signal-box, whose signalmen complained that the tunnels were sometimes so full of smoke that it was hard to see the tail lamp – a vital regulation for every passing train. Accordingly, an instruction was given for the guards of passing freight trains to blow their whistle as they passed the box to tell the signalman that the train was complete.

BATTERED BY WAVES

The signalmen at Parsons Tunnel Signal Box, north of Teignmouth in Devon, could not have been any closer to the elements, since the box was only feet away from the sea. During storms, waves would crash over the seawall and track. To screen them when gales threatened and prevent the windows being smashed by waves, shutters were provided that could be raised and lowered by chains from within the box. The signalmen were even issued with an oilskin coat and leggings once every three years. Before the doubling of the single line through the five tunnels to Dawlish, firemen trying to hand over the single-line staff (without possession of which no train could proceed) to the signalman sometimes had it dashed out of their hand by a wave, and on one occasion it was never found.

STATION WITHOUT TRAINS

Until its closure on 20 May 1968 Dartmouth in Devon had a railway station selling tickets and handling parcels, but no trains. To catch one you had to take the chain ferry across the Dart estuary to the terminus of the railway from Newton Abbot at Kingswear.

STATION GARDENS

The tradition of station gardens, thought to have begun on the North Eastern Railway, followed by the Great Western, spread rapidly. Staff at many stations have taken pride in maintaining flower-beds and hanging baskets, and an attractive floral display became almost a requisite for winning a Best Kept Station competition. The railway companies provided tools, plants and seeds and offered cash prizes for winners. The Best Kept Station competitions encouraged the green-fingered among station staff to such heights of horticultural endeavour that in the years up to the Second World War the Northern District of the London & North Eastern Railway ran excursions touring them. Remote Verney Junction was renowned in the 1950s for a garden that included a pool, dovecote, mermaid, stork, gnomes, rabbit and windmill. Stirling station's floral displays were so extensive that it had its own nursery and greenhouse.

At Shepshed in Leicestershire the station was laid out with flower-beds and rockery extending the whole length of the platform. Wooden and earthenware receptacles were filled with plants, and the platform seats were shaded by quaint rustic arbours planted with roses, clematis, honeysuckle, jasmine, hops and Virginia and canary creepers. On the Midland Railway, even platelayers' cabins beside the line commonly had a bed of roses and other flowers.

In recent years community groups have gained official blessing and encouragement to adopt stations, often resulting in a revival of horticultural pleasures for passengers.

LORD, GIVE US LUPINS

The profusion of lupins along the Bromyard branch between Worcester and Leominster was attributed to a vicar who travelled to Worcester each week and bought a packet of seeds from the penny bazaar. As he travelled back, he would throw seeds out of the window, saying 'Bless the Lord.'

RECYCLED BUILDINGS

It was extremely rare for station buildings to be anything but purpose-built. Among the few exceptions is Red Hall in Bourne, Lincolnshire, built *c.*1605, which the Bourne & Essendine Railway bought in 1860 to adapt as the ticket office and stationmaster's house. At Bardon Hill between Leicester and Burton-on-Trent an old coaching inn became the station house and passenger offices. The entrance building to Staines West in Middlesex was once a private house of *c.*1830; it was adapted to save money and retained a domestic atmosphere.

In 1881 the builders of the Mexico City–Puebla line adapted the cloisters of the former Dominican convent of San Diego, dating from 1657, to serve as the station at Cuautla, the nave becoming a warehouse for freight traffic. Scheduled trains have been replaced by buses, but the station has become a museum, part of a 1986 revival of train services as a tourist railway between Cuautla and Yecapixtla.

SCOTTISH AVALANCHE SIGNALS

The isolated signal-box at Awe Crossing between Taynuilt and Loch Awe stations on the Callander & Oban line in the western Highlands had an unusual alarm bell, linked to a 9 ft (2.7 m) high fence of wires 12 inches (31 cm) apart running through the Pass of Brander, to the west. Rocks falling on to the line would break at least one wire, causing signals protecting the approaches to the pass to go to danger and activating the bell. Before their installation, a train had been struck by a falling boulder in 1881, and the frequency with which stones were found on the track by permanent way gangs had prompted the imposition of a maximum speed through the pass of 25 mph (40 kph) by day and 12 mph (19 kph) at night. The warning system allowed the lifting of the speed restriction.

Local staff called the boulder screen 'Anderson's piano' (after the railway's remarkable company secretary/manager) because it gave a musical hum in high wind.

RAILWAY REFRESHMENT ROOMS

These facilities of wildly variable quality are almost as old as the railway. Exactly when and where the first was opened is unknown, but they were certainly a feature of railway travel before the end of the 1830s. Almost equally old are jokes and acerbic remarks about railway food, not always deserved. Some railway companies, particularly in the later 19th century, let all rooms to a single contract catering company, but others retained piecemeal lettings.

The refreshment room at Carnforth in Lancashire gained fame through its use in the making of David Lean's 1945 film *Brief Encounter*, based on a Noël Coward play. The room has been restored to its 1940s appearance and reopened serving better food.

In 1879 the station at the Lincolnshire town of Louth gained a temperance refreshment room run by the Holy Trinity Temperance Association.

CHAPTER FOUR

THE IRON HORSE

THE STEAM LOCOMOTIVE is the most demonstrative of man's mechanical creations, perfectly expressing its state through sound – almost silent but for the sizzle of hot oil in repose and emitting deafening staccato barks when being worked hard. Numerous composers, poets, novelists, painters and filmmakers have been sensitive to its drama and sought to capture its fascination. Though no one who has known the unforgettable atmosphere of a large steam engine shed will ever mistake a heritage railway for 'the real thing', the charisma of the steam locomotive has ensured that hundreds of preserved railways attract tens of millions of visitors a year. They come to enjoy the ambience of the steam railway that has enthralled generations of people, whether or not they can tell a Great Western 'King' from a 'Castle'.

A ROYAL PREROGATIVE

King Boris III of Bulgaria followed his father in demanding the right to drive the Orient Express as it passed through his country, and was on one occasion associated with a fatal accident. A blowback from the firebox engulfed the poor fireman in flames, and he fell from the footplate; Boris disregarded the loss and pressed on, determined not to lose time on so prestigious a train. Despite this, the London Midland & Scottish Railway agreed to Boris getting his hands on the regulator of one of its streamlined Pacifics on the 'Coronation Scot' between Euston and Bletchley on 5 November 1937. Local railwaymen were surprised to see him descend from the footplate wearing his trademark white overalls, designed and made for him by a Parisian tailor.

SOMETHING FOR THE POT . . .

It was quite common on branch lines, or even on main lines in the early days, for engine crews and the guard on goods trains to indulge in a spot of poaching. Between Dolyhir and New Radnor on the Great Western Railway branch from Titley, near the Welsh border, a driver used to stop to set some rabbit wires, pausing on the return journey to collect supper. Shooting estates were always good for pheasants sitting on lineside fences, irresistible targets for a well-aimed lump of coal. Even on the Lancaster & Carlisle Railway main line in the 1840s, a driver would take his whippet with him on the footplate in the hope of bagging a rabbit near Clifton & Lowther.

However, permanent way staff weren't always happy with footplate crews living off the land in this way. They were often friendly with local farmers and regarded any rabbits to be had as their perquisite. On one occasion, a train crew were in a field adjacent to the line when they were startled by their engine whistling. They returned to the footplate to discover a stern-faced inspector who had been tipped off about their diversions.

. . . OR THE FIRE

A canny shepherd north of Helmsdale on Scotland's Far North line to Wick and Thurso placed a few deceased pheasants among some birch trees close to the line and regularly altered their position. Knowing this was a good location, firemen would prepare suitable lumps of coal to try to bag one of the decoys, thereby providing the shepherd with some coal to supplement peat in the grate.

MEN AND MACHINE

It is today hard to visualise the immaculate condition in which steam locomotives were kept before the First World War. Footplate crews began their careers by joining the armies of cleaners at locomotive depots that sent both passenger and goods engines off shed with polished paint-work and gleaming brass. A celebrated class of Great Western Railway locomotive, the Dean singles, had a large brass dome on which cleaners would use powdered soot to make it gleam. The dome would then be covered with a sack until the locomotive was ready to leave the engine shed and appear in public. The pride of drivers and firemen was often fostered by each crew having their own locomotive with their names on a plate in the cab or even on the outside, as on the Midland. When locomotives were shared, tensions could arise, as recalled by the former shedmaster at Tredegar, J.M. Dunn: the two drivers who shared the large 0–8–0 freight locomotive No. 631 were greatly attached to the engine and would either wait or arrive early for a personal handover. This sometimes entailed abuse by the relieving driver for having ill-treated 'the poor little thing'.

The painstaking paint specification and elaborate lining scheme of railways such as the South Eastern & Chatham Railway combined to create a visual splendour which can still be appreciated at the National Railway Museum and heritage railways. On the Maryport & Carlisle Railway, for example, locomotives would be given four or five coats of paint protected by a coat of tallow, which would be repeated regularly.

Yet even before the First World War there was some evidence of standards of cleanliness slipping. This has been attributed partly to school-leavers choosing to go into the manufacturing sector, which offered higher wages, though not the prospects of career progression available on the railway, from cleaner to top-link driver.

No writer better captured the relationship between man and machine than Emile Zola, whose 1890 psychological thriller *La Bête Humaine* was as deeply researched as all his naturalistic novels. Zola must have had many conversations to portray so accurately the feelings of the main character, engine driver Jacques Lantier, for his locomotive *La Lison*.

WHAT'S IN A NAME?

The naming of British steam locomotives displayed varying degrees of imagination and no little learning in the case of some, especially the London & North Western with its many classically derived names. The naming of trains has been broadly successful, many becoming highly evocative, such as the *Flying Scotsman*, the *Cornish Riviera Express* and the *Pines Express*. But British Railways might have probed the name given to another train between London King's Cross and Edinburgh; the *Heart of Midlothian* is the title of a novel by Sir Walter Scott but also the nickname of the old Tolbooth prison in the Scottish capital.

AN INDIAN CURIOSITY

Visitors to the Delhi Railway Museum can see the transplanted remnant of one of the most curious railways ever built. It was created by the state engineer for the Sikh State of Patiala in the Punjab, Colonel C.W. Bowles, who employed a monorail system developed by W.J. Ewing using the ideas of the Norwich engineer and millwright William Thorold. A single rail was engaged by double-flanged wheels beneath the train, which had outrigger arms to wheels that rested on an adjacent road. The system was cheaper to build than a conventional railway and required less land, but its great advantages were flexibility – extensions could be quickly built and use sharp radius curves – and the ability to ride over rough ground.

About 60 route miles (97 km) of track were built in Patiala, and the monorail opened in stages from February 1907 to 1910, closing in 1927. Each passenger carriage had back-to-back, knifeboard seats for 20. Initially trains were hauled by some of the 300 mules maintained for military use by the Patiala State, and staging posts for the animals and muleteers were built along the way. But in March 1909 four steam locomotives were built for the railway by Orenstein & Koppel in Berlin, and it is one of these that is preserved in Delhi, along with Colonel Bowles's inspection saloon. Their rescue is thanks to a former chairman of ICI in India, Michael Satow, who was given the task of finding exhibits for the museum after he retired from the company.

MUSICAL BUFFERS

The buffers of early broad-gauge Great Western Railway locomotives were made of leather stuffed with horsehair, and after their withdrawal were sold for use as piano stools.

LION ROARS AGAIN

One of the most remarkable stories in railway preservation is the discovery of what is now one of the oldest working steam locomotives in the world. In early 1928 C.W. Reed was visiting Prince's Graving Dock in Liverpool and on a whim decided to look inside the pump room. In the gloom he saw an ancient locomotive with no nameplate, but Reed found the maker's plate and after some research discovered the locomotive's identity.

Lion was one of two locomotives ordered in 1837 from Todd, Kitson & Laird of the Airedale Foundry in Leeds by the Liverpool & Manchester Railway as 'luggage engines'. In 1859 *Lion* was sold to the Mersey Docks & Harbour Board, which mounted her on trestles in a partially stripped state for use as a pumping engine.

Her discovery seemed to startle the Board, as though it was unaware even of the existence of this venerable machine. She was decommissioned in September 1928, replaced by electric pumps and prepared for sale as scrap. Reed enlisted the help of the Liverpool Engineering Society to buy *Lion*, and Sir Henry Fowler of the London Midland & Scottish Railway agreed to restore her at Crewe works. After taking part in the centenary celebrations of the Liverpool & Manchester Railway in 1930, pulling a replica train at Wavertree, *Lion* was put on display at Liverpool's Lime Street station. The first of her three film roles was in 1937, in *Victoria the Great*, which was commissioned by Edward VIII. For the centenary celebrations of the London & Birmingham Railway at Euston station, in 1938, *Lion* steamed the mile to and from Camden engine shed, and on one occasion was driven by Colonel E. Kitson Clark, grandson of one of the founders of the builders. The threat of bombs prompted *Lion*'s removal to the greater safety of Crewe works in 1941.

In 1951 she was displayed at Exchange station in Manchester for the Festival of Britain and the same year briefly appeared in *The Lady with the Lamp*, in the scene showing Florence Nightingale returning from the Crimea, shot at Bricket Wood on the Watford–St Albans branch. But her most famous role was in 1952 in the Ealing Studios' classic *The Titfield Thunderbolt*, shot on the Camerton–Limpley Stoke branch in Somerset, when she was looked after by Westbury engine shed and its staff.

After further storage at Crewe she was loaned to Liverpool Museum before taking part in the 1980 Rainhill cavalcade to mark the 150th anniversary of the LMR. A condition survey in 1992 led to the trustees of National Museums Liverpool deciding to conserve her for museum display only, in the new Museum of Liverpool.

OUT OF HARM'S WAY

During the Second World War, the slate quarries of North Wales were used to store paintings from London art galleries. An equivalent use was made of the small engine shed at Sprouston in Roxburghshire to house the Great Western Railway locomotive *City of Truro* from York Railway Museum.

CONDITIONS ON THE FOOTPLATE

Early engine crews must have been tough to cope with the minimal protection offered by the weatherboards or minimalist cab roofs. Locomotive designers were afraid of providing comfort for the crews in case they fell asleep, a fear justified by the long hours footplatemen were expected to work. Only on tank engines and in countries where men could die of cold, such as Canada, Russia and Scandinavia, were decent cabs provided before the 20th century.

By the early 20th century some British companies were giving reasonable protection against the elements, especially the North Eastern Railway. It was even worse when a locomotive could not be turned, compelling the crew to suffer the blast of tender-first working – a low tender offered almost no protection from the elements. Just before the First World War an observer witnessed the refusal of a driver to work a train from Mablethorpe into the icy Lincolnshire winds until he had turned the engine.

DOWN A HOLE

One of the most curious fates to befall a British steam locomotive came about at Lindal ore sidings between Barrow and Ulverston in Cumbria on 22 September 1892. The area was honeycombed with mine workings, and subsidence was a common hazard. That morning Furness Railway Sharp Stewart 0–6–0 No. 115 had derailed in the sidings, and the Head Ganger had decided not to try to re-rail the locomotive without assistance from Barrow. Driver Thomas Postlethwaite and a guard were on the footplate when they saw the ballast between the sleepers disappearing and felt an unnerving sensation of the ground moving. They leapt from the footplate just in time to see the locomotive disappear chimney first into the 30 ft (9 m) deep hole, carrying Postlethwaite's jacket and gold watch with it. The 20-ton tender was recovered, but a further collapse later that day widened the hole to 75 ft (23 m), cutting parallel lines. It was not until the following spring that normal working was resumed, and even then with speed restrictions. The locomotive itself is still down there.

LEAVES ON THE LINE

Small-wheeled and light diesel and electric trains struggle with the mulch that wet leaves create on rail heads. The use of disc brakes rather than brake blocks that acted on the wheel treads has exacerbated the problem. It might be thought that the problem was unknown in the days of much heavier steam locomotives; not quite, but it was rare enough for an instance to be reported with surprise in the railway press. During the autumn of 1911 a Highland Railway goods train slipped to a halt on leaves to the south of Pitlochry, and the train had to be divided to allow any progress to be made.

RAILWAY BELLS

In contrast to many countries, British locomotives seldom carried bells as a means of warning. Exceptions could be found at docks such as Birkenhead, on Merseyside, where tank engines shunting the Docks Estate were fitted with bells behind the chimney. Across the Mersey the tolling of a bell at Pier Head presaged similar movements, which were preceded by a man walking in front with a red flag, bringing trams which crossed the dock railway on the level to a halt. The trams were heading for the Mersey ferries, and the delay elicited audible groans on the tram as passengers realised they would miss the next ferry.

Four express locomotives carried a commemorative bell: the *Royal Scot* had one for its tour of the US in 1933; Gresley A4 streamlined Pacifics *Dominion of Canada* and *Dominion of New Zealand* received bells from the countries concerned; and the Great Western Railway's *King George V* was presented with a bell by the Baltimore & Ohio Railroad after its American tour in 1927.

PIGTAILS FLYING

It was not unusual in less regulated times for admiring boys to be invited on to the footplate during station stops, or even until the next stop. One of the top-link drivers at King's Cross shed in London was the Scouser Bill Hoole. When working a northbound train one day, he took pity on two rain-soaked schoolgirls on the platform at Hitchin and invited them into the cab of A4 Pacific No. 60003 *Seagull*. As they forged along the four-track section, Hoole saw a goods train in the distance, also heading north. He invited one girl into the driver's seat and showed the other how to hold the shovel, while the enginemen hid themselves in the tender corridor. The driver of the freight turned to wave to the overtaking passenger crew and received the shock of his career as the pigtailed girls flew past.

MOOSE AHEAD

During the First World War the driver of a Canadian Pacific eastbound freight climbing to the spiral tunnels in British Columbia saw a moose ambling along the single track. No amount of whistling deterred the animal and it ventured on to the trestle viaduct just west of the tunnel. The inevitable happened: its four legs went through the gaps between the ties (sleepers) beneath the rails and the poor creature landed on its belly, legs waving over the chasm. Astonishingly, the driver and fireman managed to lift the animal and take it to the end of the viaduct, little thinking that it would do anything but dash into the forest. But no, the railway lines led into the tunnel, so there the moose went, and the crew had no option but to creep up the spiral tunnel to the upper level where the moose finally made for the trees.

UPRIGHTING A SHIP

During the devastating floods of 1953 on the east coast of England, the supports for two ships in dry dock at Immingham were washed away by the force of the flood-water, causing the vessels to topple on to their sides. When the water was pumped out, the magnitude of the task of righting them was apparent. Steel pillars were welded to the hull sides and steel ropes attached to them. These were passed through a series of pulley blocks, which had the effect of magnifying by 14 times a pull on the rope. The steel rope was attached to two steam locomotives (O4 2–8–0s) on a

LOOKING FOR WASHOUTS

During the wet season in Nigeria, it was necessary for a driver or foreman platelayer to ride on the buffer beam of locomotives to watch out for evidence of soil being washed away from the track.

line beside the dock. Using radio links between a control room and the locomotives, they slowly exerted force on the rope as water was let into the dry dock. In half an hour the first ship was upright again.

LOCOMOTIVE HIRE IN 1913

The Vale of Rheidol Railway experienced such heavy traffic in the summer of 1912 when army training camps were set up at Devils's Bridge, east of Aberystwyth, that its three locomotives were unable to cope, so it hired *Palmerston* from the Festiniog Railway. The hire charge was £2 a day. Her driver, David Davies or 'Old Dafydd', was so attached to his engine and reluctant to let any of the VoR staff near her that he slept in the swept-out tender each night. *Palmerston* was hired again in 1913, but this time a VoR driver got his hands on her when Old Dafydd wasn't about and took her up the line. All went well until the horseshoe bend at Erwtomau, when *Palmerston* slipped so badly that a side rod was bent. She was hired again in 1914, 1915, 1921 and 1922, the locomotive being conveyed by the Cambrian Railways from the exchange sidings at Minffordd to those at Aberystwyth.

DRAWING BOARD TO SERVICE IN SIX MONTHS

In the 21st century it can take many months or even years simply to gain the necessary approvals for a completed train to enter public service. Things were rather different in the 1930s. The London & North Eastern Railway's renown chief mechanical engineer Sir Nigel Gresley had visited Germany in 1934 to see the diesel 'Flying Hamburger', then the world's fastest train, averaging 77.4 mph (124.5 kph) over the 178 miles (286 km) between Berlin and Hamburg. Gresley returned convinced that steam could do just as well.

The London & North Eastern Railway had decided that it would introduce a new streamlined service between London and Newcastle to coincide with the 25th anniversary of the coronation of George V in September 1935, with the name 'Silver Jubilee'. Approval to build four locomotives to operate the new train was given only in March. Although the Drawing Office had done some preliminary work, design work took some months and it was not until 26 June that the frames were laid at Doncaster works. The completed prototype, *Silver Link*, left the works 74 days later, on 7 September. The precursor of *Mallard*, the future holder of the world speed record for steam, *Silver Link* had a revolutionary air-smooth shape and three-tone grey livery that grabbed newspaper headlines.

Two weeks of running in preceded a high-speed run and brake test to prepare for a publicity and press train on the 27th when *Silver Link* reached 112 mph (180 kph) at Arlesey, 6 miles (9.6 km) north of Hitchin. Three days later the scheduled 'Silver Jubilee' service began with the 10am departure from Newcastle. For the next fortnight *Silver Link* operated all workings, covering 536.6 miles (863.4 km) a day at an average speed of 67 mph (108 kph).

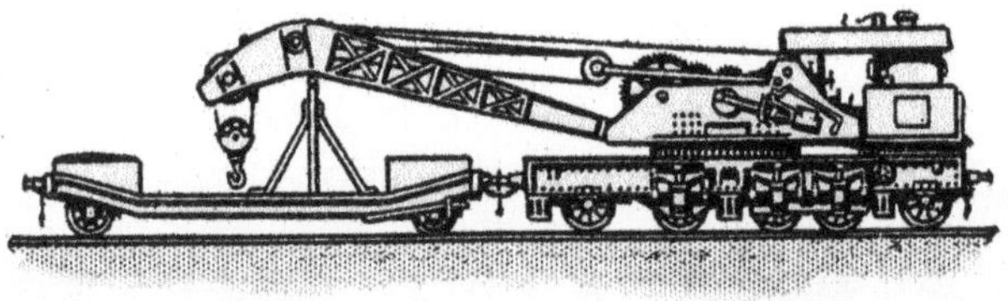

LOOK AT ME!

The first Southern Railway four-cylinder 4–6–0 *Lord Nelson* appeared in 1926, in response to the need for a locomotive that could haul 500-ton trains at an average speed of 55 mph (88 kph). Its tractive effort enabled the Southern's publicity department to produce a poster proclaiming the 'Most powerful passenger engine in Great Britain', even if the arcane calculations behind the boast meant little in reality. To add to the publicity, it is said that drivers were asked to sound the whistle for longer when passing through major stations to attract attention. One driver was severely reprimanded when he overdid the request and provided Ashford, Kent, with a mile-long scream.

RURAL EXCHANGE

A passenger on a London Paddington to South Wales express in the early 1950s overheard an innocent misunderstanding on a country station platform when the train made an unscheduled stop. The train's locomotive, a 'Castle', had given signs that it would not complete the journey and it slowly came to a halt at a quiet station. The platform's only occupant was a youthful porter who was transfixed with surprise at the sight of this lordly express honouring his station with a visit. The driver was leaning out of the cab and looking for someone to order up a new mount. 'New engine,' he shouted, catching sight of the porter, 'new engine.' The porter was evidently unfamiliar with engine types, but he may have heard talk of the new 'Britannias' and their rather too frequent failings. 'Is it?' he called back.

TELLING THE WORLD IN 1870

Snowdonia was in 1870 the unlikely setting for a remarkable demonstration of new technology, attracting visitors from around the world when international travel was slow and difficult. The occasion was the first public display of a locomotive designed using the principles of a patent granted to Robert Fairlie in 1864, for an articulated locomotive with two sets of wheels and motion. The locomotive, No. 7 *Little Wonder*, had been built by Fairlie's father-in-law George England at the Hatcham Ironworks in New Cross, London, for the Festiniog Railway. Fairlie had a well-developed sense of the importance of good public relations and arranged with the FR's progressive manager, Charles Spooner, for comparative trials between *Little Wonder* and previous tank engines built by England for the FR.

The trials were held in February 1870 and were attended by the 3rd Duke of Sutherland and an Imperial Commission from Russia headed by Count Alekseyevich Bobrinskoy, who was Minister of Transportation from 1868 to 1871, as well as engineers from France, Germany, Hungary, India, Mexico, Norway, Sweden and Switzerland. The trials showed the overwhelming superiority of Fairlie's concept. On the 12th, Spooner gave a paper in the Oakeley Arms Hotel in Tan-y-Bwlch, where many of the delegates were staying; he outlined the benefits of combining a narrow gauge with Fairlie's patent locomotive. Spooner gained a gold medal from the Tsar, and Fairlie won locomotive orders for Russia's Imperial Livny Railway, the Iquique Railway in Chile, the Chemin de Fer de la Vendée and the Nassjo–Oskarshamn Railway in Sweden.

The following year the FR was visited by General William Jackson Palmer while on his honeymoon. He had set up the Denver & Rio Grande Railway the previous year, and the visit convinced him of the advantages of the narrow gauge, encouraging him to settle for the 3 ft gauge which became so common for secondary systems in the US.

FOUR-LEGGED FRIENDS

Of all collecting dogs the greatest traveller was probably a Scottish Collie named Help (1882–91), who collected £1,004 for the Railway Servants Orphan Fund. His activities were the idea of a guard on the night boat train of the London Brighton & South Coast Railway, John Climpson, who trained Help. The dog travelled throughout Scotland, Ireland and Wales and twice crossed the Channel to France. He wore a handsome collar, bearing a silver tag reading 'I am Help the railway dog of England, and travelling agent for the orphans of railwaymen who are killed on duty', and also carried the address of the London offices to which interested persons could send donations. When Help died at Newhaven, Climpson had him preserved and put in a glass case on the platform at Brighton.

THE FIRST WHISTLE

The whistle of the steam locomotive was a sound that permeated urban and rural life for a century and a half. The timbre of whistles varied enormously, from the shrill to the deep hooter, but it was an evocative sound that many thought as pleasing in the landscape as birdsong. As well as acting as a warning, whistle codes were used as routing signals to shunting staff and signalmen. Unofficially they were used by enginemen to alert their wives that they were back. At the Yorkshire railway colony of Hellifield, every wife knew her husband's poppety-pop, and this would be the signal for her to start preparing a meal.

The whistle's inventor was a Cornishman, Adrian Stephens, who designed and fitted a whistle to a stationary boiler at the Dowlais Ironworks in Glamorgan in about 1831. Its purpose and how it was transferred to the railway remain uncertain, but a sketch of the whistle found its way to the Liverpool & Manchester Railway by 1835. A whistle is recorded on the Newcastle & Carlisle Railway by June 1836, in France the following year and in the US by 1838. The Leicester & Swannington Railway appears to have found an independent route to a steam-powered warning device; a 'steam trumpet' was introduced after an accident at a road crossing on 4 May 1833, though this may have simply been a different name for a whistle.

Stephens's whistle can be seen in the Cyfartha Castle Museum & Art Gallery at Merthyr Tydfil, the Mid-Glamorgan town where he died in straitened circumstances in 1871.

ROUND AND ROUND

The turntable at Hawes Junction on the Settle & Carlisle Railway was in such an exposed position that one day in December 1900 the wind caught a locomotive and set it spinning like a top. The engine crew had to throw shovelfuls of cinders on to the perimeter rail to bring it to a halt. It is not certain whether it was this incident or the need to protect the pit from drifting snow that gave rise to the turntable being given a stockade of vertical sleepers, but it was certainly a feature unique in Britain.

BREAKFAST ON THE SHOVEL

Many swear there is no better way to have a fry-up than off a shovel in the firebox, a time-honoured tradition of footplate crews. After a battle through the snow on the South Wales Heads of the Valley line in 1922, the crew on an engine at Nantybwch were looking forward to tucking into the sizzling eggs and ham when one of them caught the blower handle, creating a sudden suction on the fire. The eggs and ham flew off the shovel and were flattened on the tube plate, eliciting some choice language.

MISPLACED PRIORITIES

Well over a thousand steam locomotives have been preserved in Britain, but there have been disgraceful instances of locomotives set aside for posterity being summarily cut up for paltry reasons. Paradoxically, the Great Western Railway was the worst culprit, despite having a longer and more colourful history than any other major British railway. Two locomotives had been set aside before the broad gauge was abolished in 1892: *North Star* of 1837 and *Lord of the Isles*, built in 1851 and exhibited at the Great Exhibition. Both were scrapped in 1906 while George Jackson Churchward was Chief Mechanical Engineer.

The exigencies of war demand sacrifice, but the scrap drives of the wars have been shown to be of little or no value. A casualty of the First

World War was Shrewsbury & Chester Railway 2–2–2 No. 14, which had been kept at Stafford Road shed, Wolverhampton.

Another Swindon protégé, William Stanier, showed as little regard for history as Churchward when he took over as Chief Mechanical Engineer of the London Midland & Scottish Railway, cutting up Midland double-framed Kirtley 0–6–0 No. 421 of 1856, Kirtley 2–4–0 No. 156A, Johnson 0–4–4T No. 1226 and North London Railway 4–4–0T No. 6 without hesitation when space in the paint shop was needed.

PICKING UP WATER

The necessity for steam locomotives to stop at periodic intervals to take on more water was a major handicap in accelerating schedules. To overcome this, the Locomotive Superintendent of the London & North Western Railway, John Ramsbottom, devised a metal trough placed centrally between the rails from which a lowered scoop mounted beneath the locomotive tender could pick up water. He patented the idea in 1860, and the first water troughs came into use that

RAILWAY SIGNS

A notice at Stalybridge Joint Station in Cheshire warned: 'ALL PERSONS FOUND TRESPASSING OR LOITERING ON THESE PREMISES ARE LIABLE TO BE TAKEN INTO CUSTODY TO BE DEALT WITH ACCORDING TO LAW.'

year at Mochdre on the North Wales coast line, specifically to improve the running times of the Irish Mail train.

The most exposed water troughs in Britain were on the Settle & Carlisle line between Hawes Junction and Rise Hill Tunnel. In winter, steam raisers from Hellifield were sent to a lineside boiler to heat the troughs, and gangers had to chip and shovel ice off the rails; each train splashed water over the rails which immediately froze. A build-up would have made the line unusable.

The idea of water troughs was adopted in France and the US.

CHAPTER FIVE

ON THE TRAIN

COMPETENTLY PROVIDED train travel is widely regarded as a most civilised way of getting from A to B. It's generally stress-free and most importantly it isn't the waste of time that journeys by car entail. Passengers can work, read, think and sleep. It's a more sociable way to travel, and few passengers will not have stories of convivial conversations as a result of chance meetings on trains. Remarkably, passenger numbers in many countries are soaring as a second railway age gathers pace. The consequences of the delusional reliance on road transport have become ever more apparent, and governments throughout the world are rebuilding urban rail networks and constructing new high-speed lines. At the same time, the sheer pleasure of travel by train has seen a growth in holidays by rail, both to reach destinations and using trains as mobile hotels.

CANADIAN NATIONAL RAILWAYS

THE PLEASURE OF EATING ON TRAINS

It is almost impossible on British railways today to enjoy a freshly cooked meal served in a manner befitting a restaurant, with white napery, silverware and glass. Yet before the First World War, such facilities were taken for granted, even by third-class passengers. The Midland Railway alone had 115 dining-cars in service in 1911. Among the 12 carriages of the Great Eastern Railway's 'Norfolk Coast Express' in 1911 were enough dining-cars for 72 third- and 36 first-class passengers to be served with a meal simultaneously (see page 126 for the abolishment of second class). The level of service offered by the GER enticed 184,000 passengers to use the restaurant cars in 1910. Even during the First World War restaurant cars were provided on trains over the East Suffolk line from Ipswich to Lowestoft and Yarmouth, and to Sheringham on the Norfolk coast. A second- or third-class wartime dinner menu might consist of consommé Macédoine, roast sirloin with Yorkshire pudding, roast and boiled potatoes and spring cabbage, gooseberry tart and custard followed by cheese and biscuits with watercress. Price 2s 6d (12½p). For an additional shilling, the first-class menu would be identical but with the addition of a fish course of boiled salmon with caper sauce and cucumber and the option of Orleans pudding.

SLEEPING ON TRAINS

Credit for the first sleeping car goes to the Cumberland Valley Railroad in Pennsylvania, which introduced the service between Harrisburg and Chambersburg in 1837. The 'beds' were adapted from seats. A similarly makeshift arrangement, using two poles with webbing between them, was implemented in Britain the following year, by the London & Birmingham and Grand Junction railways. The first purpose-built sleeping car is thought to have been built in 1857 at Hamilton, Ontario, on Canada's Great Western Railway.

ON EXPENSES

When Guy Burgess, later exposed as a spy, was upbraided by the BBC for claiming first-class travel to a funeral in Cambridge, he replied in writing: 'Incidentally, I was wearing my best clothes, which matter for such an occasion. Incidentally also, I normally travel first class.'

THE CRAFT OF CARRIAGE BUILDING

Only between the two world wars did the use of steel in carriage bodies become common, and even then steel panels were often placed over wood frames. Before the First World War carriage bodies were largely built of wood, calling for very different skills in the workforce and in the sourcing of materials. The North Eastern Railway's carriage works in York had a huge timber drying shed and wood yard to ensure that the woods it used were both properly seasoned and in stock. It sourced oak of various kinds from Britain, the US, Russia, Poland and Austria; mahogany from central America, Tabasco and Cuba; teak from eastern India and Burma; walnut from southern Europe; rosewood from central America and

Jamaica; satinwood from the East and West Indies; sycamore from Britain; ash from Britain and Hungary; Kauri pine from New Zealand; jarrah wood from Australia; yellow pine from Canada; fir from Prussia, Poland and Russia; pitch-pine from North America; and spruce from Norway and Russia.

Upholstery was stuffed with horsehair and processed in the Hair Teasing Shop. In the Painting Shop carriages were given 13 coats of paint, followed by five coats of varnish in a separate workshop.

MAKE USE OF TIME, LET NOT ADVANTAGE SLIP

Train journeys provide the solitary passenger with the opportunity and freedom to read or work. Anthony Trollope wrote the greater part of *Barchester Towers* and subsequent novels during his railway journeys in south-west England in the 1850s on behalf of the Post Office. During a General Election campaign in the 1860s, Gladstone spent train journeys translating the *Odes* of Horace, which he later published. Prokofiev used train journeys across North America while on a concert tour in 1930 to study Beethoven's quartets, in preparation for writing his first string quartet, commissioned by the Library of Congress. Appropriately, Vivian Ellis composed *Coronation Scot* while on the train between Paddington and Taunton in 1938. John le Carré started writing the Smiley novels on the train between Great Missenden and London. There would have been no Harry Potter but for train journeys: not only did J.K. Rowling's parents meet on a train between London King's Cross and

Arbroath, but the idea for Harry Potter came to her on the train between Manchester and London.

UNDER HIS OWN STEAM

The journey to work of Henry Schneider from his Lake Windermere home at Belsfield House (now the Belsfield Hotel) must have been one of the most agreeable commutes in Britain. Every morning he left home by walking down through the garden to his private pier, preceded by his butler carrying a silver salver, and to his waiting steam launch *Esperance*, on which he had breakfast on his way to Lakeside at the southern end of the lake. There he boarded his private carriage (he was a director of the Furness Railway) for the journey by rail to Barrow, where he was a partner in the Barrow Haematite Iron and Steel Company, which was then the largest Bessemer-process steelworks in the world, employing more than 5,000 workers. The SL *Esperance* was the model for Captain Flint's houseboat in Arthur Ransome's *Swallows and Amazons* and is now preserved in the Windermere Steamboat Museum.

GILDING THE LILY

It is a commonplace that standards of train catering and facilities for first-class passengers have declined, but few trains could ever have matched the facilities of a dining-car train of 1901 on the Niagara Falls route of the Michigan Central. It had a parlour-car and a library-car with a stenographer and typist as well as newspapers and the principal magazines. At the other end of the car was a barber's shop. In the dining-car there was an extensive menu for one dollar. At three of the stops on an eight-hour journey, boys came on board and gave each passenger a fine rose or two or a bunch of flowers.

THE FIRST PULLMAN

The carriages of George Mortimer Pullman (1831–97) became a byword for luxury on the rails in many parts of the world. The very first purpose-built Pullman car, *Pioneer*, built in 1865, shot to fame in May 1865 when it carried the widow of Abraham Lincoln from Chicago to the President's birthplace at Springfield, Illinois. The funeral train had left Washington D.C. on 21 April and passed through 180 cities and seven states. At each scheduled stop the coffin was unloaded on to a decorated hearse and taken to a public building where people could pay their respects. When the train reached Chicago on 2 May, Mrs Lincoln collapsed under the strain, and *Pioneer* was added to the train so that she could complete the journey in privacy. It was perfect publicity for Pullman's vision for luxury train travel; at the station of Joliet, Illinois, alone, 12,000 people gathered beside the line at midnight to watch the train pass by. Sadly this historic car was withdrawn and broken up at Pullman, Illinois, in 1900, its last duty having been to convey the 43rd Infantry Division across the continent on its way to the Philippines during the war between the US and Spain.

The first British railway company to enter into an agreement with Pullman was the Midland, which introduced a Pullman car on 1 June 1874. The train left Bradford (Market Street) at 8.20am for London St Pancras, arriving at 2.05pm. The open saloon rather than compartments was not welcomed by many travellers, but soon most railway companies with long-distance trains were operating expresses with at least one Pullman car in the rake of carriages.

By 1930 the Pullman Car Company had over 10,000 cars operating worldwide and with over 100,000 travellers accommodated each night had a claim to be the world's largest hotel.

SMARTER SOLDIERS

In 1912 what was probably the best-equipped laundry-car ever built was made in Hanover and put into service on Russian government railways for the use of Imperial troops. It contained a steam boiler, condensing tank, feed pump, injector, steam engine, cold and hot water tanks, soda cleansing medium, washing machine, draining box, centrifugal dryers, mangle, fans, ventilator and disinfector, ironing board, heaters and storage. One can't imagine it had much use after 1917.

FIRST ELECTRICALLY LIT CARRIAGE

The first British carriage to be lit by electricity was the London Brighton & South Coast Railway Pullman drawing-room car *Beatrice*, completed in October 1881. Its success encouraged provision of electric light in all carriages of the Pullman Express Limited, which began service the following December between London Victoria and Brighton.

I'M ON THE PHONE

Telephones on trains were a briefly appreciated facility of the 1980s until the mobile phone killed demand. But the first telephone was installed on a British train in 1910 when the London Brighton & South Coast Railway carried out a trial between Horley and Three Bridges. There was a space of 18 in (46 cm) between wires laid on the ground and a wire on the train. It was so successful that the LBSCR General Manager planned to install the system on the 'Southern Belle'.

RAILWAY SIGNS

The Oregon Railway & Navigation Company advised that its 'MIXED TRAINS HAVE ACCOMMODATION FOR PASSENGERS, WHO WISH TO ASSUME THE ADDITIONAL RISK OF ACCIDENT'.

TO BRIGHTON IN STYLE

The 'Brighton Belle', the electric Pullman train that linked Brighton with London Victoria between 1933 and 1972, had a unique ventilation system controlled by photo-electric cells which prevented smoke (from steam locomotives) penetrating the interiors. The train was famous for the kippers served at breakfast, but on one occasion someone burnt the kippers before departure from Brighton. The fire brigade got to work with such enthusiasm that they pulled half the carriage to pieces in trying to locate the source of the fire. In its final year, kippers were 11p each, with grilled sirloin steak with tomatoes, peas and French fries available at 95p.

FOUR-LEGGED FRIENDS

A Siccawei Airedale named Laddie began collecting at Waterloo station in 1949 and after raising over £6,000 was retired, appropriately, to the Southern Railwaymen's Home for Old People at Woking. Upon his death, he was stuffed and placed in a glass case and continued collecting on Platform 8 at Wimbledon station. Laddie is now at the National Railway Museum at York.

METRO-LAND

Between 1 June 1910 and 1939 the Metropolitan Railway operated two umber and white Pullman cars, *Mayflower* and *Galatea*, linking Aldgate with Chesham and Aylesbury. *Mayflower* had a crimson deep pile carpet and armchairs covered in crimson morocco arranged around eight glass-topped tables lit by tiny portable electroliers 'of a very chaste design', as one writer put it. The blinds were of green silk damask, and the ormolu baggage racks had panels of brass trelliswork. Each accommodated 19 passengers and their function was to allow City men an extra half-hour in bed and to take their breakfast 'quietly and comfortably' on the move, while a late evening departure after the theatre would allow supper to be enjoyed on the way home. On Saturdays golfers could reach the courses served by the Metropolitan and have lunch on the way. The Pullmans could be used by any first-class ticket holder on payment of 6d (2½p) between London and Rickmansworth and a shilling (5p) for stations further north.

STYLE IN RAILROAD CARS

In the 1959 film *Some Like It Hot*, Marilyn Monroe tells Tony Curtis that she wants a man with his own railroad car. This had its heyday in the US between 1870 and the First World War, when hundreds of these cars carried plutocrats around the country in unparalleled opulence. No expense was spared: lighting by chandelier, water through gold taps, deep carpets underfoot. Their use declined from the 1920s, but some of these cars have been preserved privately and in public museum collections.

The decade after the Second World War was the last hurrah of the American passenger train, before the railroads threw in the towel in the face of subsidised roads and air transport. The final flourish produced trains with extraordinary panache. Between 1941 and 1968 the Southern Pacific operated an all-sleeper train named 'The Lark' over the 470 miles (756 km) between San Francisco and Los Angeles, later hauled by streamlined locomotives in a striking orange, red, black and silver Daylight livery. In the centre of the train was an articulated, triple-unit Lark Club lounge over 200 ft (60 m) long; one unit contained a kitchen and crew space, the centre unit a 48-seat dining-room, and the third a bar with seats for 48. The space could be converted overnight to serve 96 breakfasts in the morning or as a two-unit cocktail lounge.

In 1952 the Pennsylvania Railroad introduced four new sets of carriages for its 'Senator' and 'Congressional' expresses between New York and Washington. They were equipped with such novel facilities as telephone booths and conference spaces. Each had a dining-car, a coffee shop/cocktail bar and a buffet in the tail-end observation car.

A bar car on the Great Northern 'Empire Builder' was fitted out to resemble a pioneer's log cabin, and the Chicago-based Rock Island Line (immortalised in song by Leadbelly and Lonnie Donegan) had a Mexican-style Fiesta Car with striped awnings.

DOUBLE-DECK LUXURY

A feature of early Indian railways was the use of double-deck carriages for scheduled trains, with the passengers riding in the upper level and their servants below. In 1863 the Governor of Bombay had a similar vehicle built with a sitting-room/bedroom and an adjacent dining-room.

CAMPING COACHES

An imaginative use for old carriages was to convert them into holiday homes and place them in spare sidings at scenic stations, which the holidaymakers would of course reach by train as part of the package. They reflected the inter-war growth of camping and activity holidays. The London & North Eastern Railway introduced them in 1933, with 10 on offer. Both the London Midland & Scottish and Great Western railways copied the idea the following year with 'caravans' and 'camp coaches' respectively, and the Southern followed suit in 1935.

During the war they provided temporary accommodation for railway staff and other users, but revival of their original use after the war was slow until 1952. By the summer of 1956 British Railways was offering 187 camping coaches, with the largest number on the Western Region. Surprisingly some of the locations, such as Aber on the North Wales coast and Hest Bank in Lancashire, were on main lines, so the occupants would have had mail, newspaper and goods trains rumbling past all night.

Alone among the pre-nationalisation companies, the GWR, typically, had maintained a policy of one coach at each location, guaranteeing some privacy. The LMS had no such scruples, packing 36 vehicles into the colony at Heysham in Lancashire and 30 at Conway Morfa in North Wales. After nationalisation, the Western Region in 1956 reneged on such niceties, placing a second coach at Dawlish Warren in south Devon, and by 1963 there were nine there.

The number declined from the mid 1960s as suitable staffed stations diminished, and they were last occupied by the public in 1971. A few were kept on for the use of railway families, notably a cluster of former Pullman coaches at Marazion in Cornwall and the coaches at Dawlish Warren.

SIGHTSEEING FROM THE TRAIN

Carriages to help passengers enjoy the passing view developed with 19th-century tourism. The Bödeli Railway, opened in 1874 to connect piers on each side of the isthmus of Interlaken in Switzerland, had wine-red double-deck coaches with longitudinal seats along the upper level so that views of the Bernese Oberland could be appreciated to the full. A large model of one can be seen in the Transport Museum in Luzern.

An 'observation sleeper' was devised and patented by T.J. McBride of Winnipeg, Manitoba, in 1891. The first dome car was introduced on the Canadian Pacific Railway in 1902. In the US it was a ride on a diesel locomotive through Glenwood Canyon in Colorado that inspired Cyrus Osborn to encourage the Chicago, Burlington & Quincy Railroad to rebuild a Budd car with dome and longitudinal seats. Dome cars have become a major feature of North American leisure train travel, with the largest fleet operated by VIA in Canada.

So that passengers in its 'Strata Domes' could enjoy the landscape even at night, the Baltimore & Ohio Railroad went so far as fitting four powerful searchlights that could sweep the countryside.

GRAND TRUNK RAILWAY,

BUFFALO AND GODERICH DIVISION.

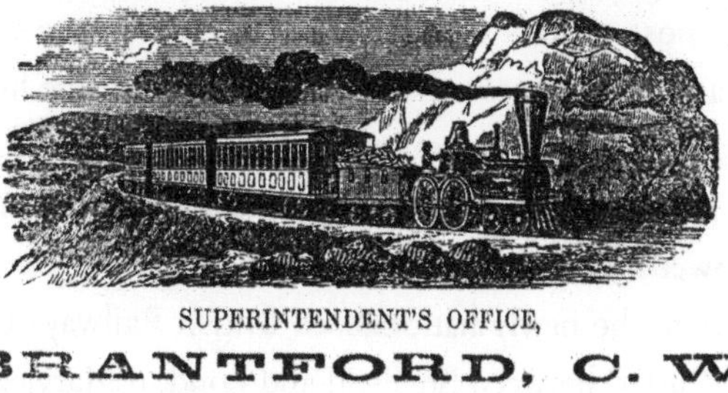

SUPERINTENDENT'S OFFICE,

BRANTFORD, C. W.

PRESIDENTIAL PALACES

Presidents in charge of countries with railway systems have seldom forgone the opportunity to have a luxurious carriage built for their use. It takes quite an extraordinary carriage to stand out from the crowd, but one was 'presented' to the President of the Argentine Republic by the Metropolitan Amalgamated Railway Carriage & Wagon Co. of Birmingham. The carriage was displayed at the exhibition in Buenos Aires in May 1910 to mark the centenary of Argentine independence, seemingly in the hope that it would lead to substantial orders for the company's products.

The carriage was unusually long at 78 ft (23.7 m) and rode on six-wheel bogies. Recessed entrance doors were placed centrally. One corridor led to a white-painted Louis XVI-inspired day saloon with an ornate fireplace and alcove for a mantelpiece clock above it. Through a door on the other side of the fireplace was a bedroom with bathroom of marble-lined walls to waist level. Off the other end of the corridor were two bedrooms with shared bathroom, wood-panelled study and attendant's room. Heating pipes were covered with ornamental brass casings, and electric fans were provided for use in hot weather.

PUBS ON WHEELS

Some of the most curious railway catering vehicles were eight windowless tavern cars which appeared in 1949, decorated inside like a pub with mock Tudor décor including real oak beams, timber-framed panels and settles. The idea even extended to the outside paint scheme with faux brickwork lower sides and timber-framing above. They were extremely unpopular when the newly nationalised British Railways used them on 'The Master Cutler' between Sheffield and London Marylebone in 1949; they had been designed for short-distance runs by the Southern Railway, but the attempt to introduce a novel element to railway catering was marred by its execution, especially the gimmickry and lack of windows. Their deficiencies were even raised in the House of Commons by Tom Driberg. Despite a spirited defence by a young James Callaghan, they were soon withdrawn in the face of such widespread criticism.

AFTERNOON TEA THROUGH CENTRAL WALES

The London Midland & Scottish Railway operated three tea cars created from London & North Western Railway third-class corridor coaches. Between the wars one of them worked on the 10.25am from Swansea Victoria to Shrewsbury over the gloriously scenic Central Wales line, being detached at Craven Arms for the return south on the 3.17pm.

THE FIRST DINING-CAR

The first British dining-car service was introduced by the Great Northern Railway, in partnership with the Pullman Car Company, on 1 November 1879 when the Pullman diner *Prince of Wales* left Leeds Central at 10am for London King's Cross.

ASSOCIATION BY SMELL

Trains run primarily for Clydeside shipyard workers before the First World War were not to be recommended for other passengers. A writer was forced to catch one to keep an appointment at a Glasgow tea room and recalled 'its unforgettable vileness . . . due to a combination of strong tobacco and the potent stench of shipyard tallow'. His fears that the aromas might have clung to his clothes were confirmed when on arrival at the tea room he was asked whether he had fallen into the Clyde.

PASSENGERS CARRIED FREE – BUT NOT ACCESSORIES

The Liskeard & Caradon Railway was built primarily to serve Cornish copper mines and quarries, but between 1860 and 1896 passenger accommodation was provided even though the Board of Trade had not passed the railway for such traffic. The railway got round this legal nicety by giving away free passes once you had bought a ticket for your hat, walking stick or umbrella. A notice at Tokenbury station reminded passengers that 'all passes are issued gratuitously, but solely on the conditions that . . . the use of any free pass . . . shall be taken as evidence of an agreement with the Directors that neither the Company nor the Directors or their servants are to be responsible for any injury or damage which may occur to any person travelling by a free pass through accident, delay, or otherwise whether occasioned by any act or neglect of the Company or its servants or otherwise, or for the loss or damage to property however caused.'

NO PETROL ON BOARD

Even in 1910 the railway-operated Newhaven–Dieppe route was becoming popular with motorists taking their car to the Continent, charged according to the length of the wheel-base. It was a regulation that all petrol tanks must be emptied before going on board.

OBLIVION IN OFFICE

Stanley Baldwin had an interest in railways that went beyond his directorship of the Great Western Railway, and he claimed that the motor car was responsible for more human misery than any other invention. (He was also the last prime minister who never flew.) There is a story, perhaps apocryphal, that during his second term as Prime Minister, he was on a train when he observed the man opposite staring at him. After a few moments, the man tapped him on the knee and said, 'You're Baldwin, aren't you? Harrow '84', referring to the famous public school. He seemed satisfied with Baldwin's assent, but a few minutes later the man again tapped the Prime Minister on the knee and said, 'Tell me, what are you doing now?'

When another erstwhile director of the GWR, Sir Harold Macmillan, was travelling on the Western Region of British Railways after he had ceased to be Prime Minister in 1963, he commented on the attentive service and enquired whether all former premiers were so treated. 'Oh no, sir,' came the reply, 'only former directors of the Great Western.'

TRAPPED IN THE USA

As part of the New York World Fair in 1939, the London Midland & Scottish Railway sent the 'Coronation Scot', comprising a blue and silver streamlined locomotive and eight matching coaches. It made a 3,000-mile (4,800 km) tour of 14 states before war was declared. It was decided not to risk shipping the train back, the locomotive being put into store until 1943, when it was finally returned. The carriages did not return until 1946, having spent the war at Jacksonville, Indiana, where they were used as living quarters for US army officers.

DETERMINED REVENUE PROTECTION

In the days before corridor carriages, it was obviously impossible for the guard or ticket inspectors to work their way through the train. Ticket platforms outside large stations enabled collectors to check tickets on incoming trains, but Charles Dickens described the alternative on a

Calais–Paris train during a stormy night. The guard worked his way along the outside of the moving train and held on with his elbows inside the window, standing 'in such a whirlwind that I grip him fast by the collar and feel it next to manslaughter to let him go'.

LONDON–EDINBURGH IN THE 1930s

The rolling stock used on the 'Flying Scotsman' in 1930 included a hairdressing salon and a Louis XVI-style restaurant, while one carriage enabled passengers to listen to the radio through headsets and see radio-photographs of such events as the finish of the Derby.

CLASS DISTINCTION

The attitude of some early railway companies to the carriage of the 'lower orders' was encapsulated in the remark by the chairman of the London & Birmingham Railway, George Carr Glyn, that allowing third-class passengers into all its trains 'would be considered generally objectionable to the other passengers; and that the habits and needs of those who travel by the third class trains are sufficiently met by the accommodation we now afford.' The poor conditions in open wagons encouraged the creation of parliamentary trains, introduced in 1844 in an endeavour to improve the travelling lot of third-class passengers. They were satirised in Gilbert and Sullivan's *The Mikado*:

The idiot who, in railway carriages
Scribbles on window-panes
We only suffer
To ride on a buffer
On parliamentary trains.

RAISING CARRIAGE STANDARDS

The man most associated with improving the lot of the third-class passenger was James Allport (1811–92), who abolished second class and relabelled such carriages third class when he was General Manager of the Manchester Sheffield & Lincolnshire Railway between 1850 and 1853. He did the same on the Midland Railway in 1875, and the higher standards were reflected in the introduction of third-class dining-cars, though the Great Eastern Railway was the first company to introduce them, in 1891. Developing third-class travel through better facilities was a policy widely adopted by other railways, and Allport was the first railway manager to be knighted. He died in the Midland Grand Hotel at St Pancras, 'a peculiarly appropriate halting place for one who has done so much to raise the Midland to its present powerful and prosperous condition', as the *Railway News* expressed it.

Allport's rearrangement of classes survived into the nationalised era. When British Railways announced that all third-class carriages would become second class from 3 June 1956, the only three-class service was the Continental boat trains, which became two classes only from the same date.

RAILWAY PARLANCE ABROAD

A mid-19th-century conversation-guide-cum-phrasebook published in Paris gave travellers helpful Spanish, French and Italian translations of such remarks as: 'Let us make haste. We have only a quarter of an hour to spare. Let us hasten to have our trunks booked. I am going to deposit a casket of jewels and my valuables.'

A suggested question for use during a visit to the railway was: 'Why are those pits made between the rails?' To which the following reply might be expected: 'To allow the engineer to survey and repair the engine without laying it over on its side.'

TRAINS DE LUXE

The two decades before the First World War were in some ways the apogee of the opulent trains of that extraordinary organisation, the International Sleeping Car Company or, to give it its full and more romantic name, La

Compagnie Internationale des Wagons-Lits et des Grands Express Européens. CIWL's gold emblem could be seen as far afield as China and eastern Russia.

Its most famous train was the Orient Express, which first ran between the Gare de Strasbourg (now the Gare de l'Est) in Paris and Constantinople on 4 October 1883, cutting the journey time between them by 30 hours. The carriages were panelled in teak, walnut and mahogany and decorated with Gobelins tapestries. Passengers sat on leather seats, slept in silk sheets, drank out of crystal and were served by waiters in powdered wigs, tail coats, breeches and silk stockings. The wigs were abandoned when a passenger complained of powder in his soup.

The train became associated with diplomats, couriers with diplomatic bags, spies, crooks and courtesans. The ambience of the famed continental expresses like the Orient Express was thought so redolent of illicit sex that a celebrated brothel near Parc Monceau in Paris re-created the décor and sounds of a Wagons-Lits sleeping-car.

CIWL soon ventured beyond Europe. The Nord Express linking Paris Nord, Berlin, Warsaw, Riga and St Petersburg began in 1896, with a change into a train of Russian 5 ft gauge at Eydtkuhnen (now Chernyshevskoye). The train built for the Trans-Siberian International Express was the sensation of the Paris Universal Exhibition of 1900. Each carriage for just eight people was in a different style – Louis XVI, Greek, French Empire, Chinese – and each had its own drawing-room and smoking-room. It had a music room with full-size grand piano, a library with books in four languages, a hairdressing salon finished in white sycamore, a gym with weights, exercise bicycle and rowing machine, a chapel car and a fully equipped darkroom. By 1914 CIWL had 32 luxury trains in service, but most ceased operation during the First World War, to be revived afterwards in usually less ostentatious form.

INDIA FOR BATHS

The first baths in carriages for public service were installed in India as early as the 1860s, far in advance of Europe and North America. By February 1873 Thomas Cook was hiring a saloon carriage with sleeping berths, baths and closets which was used as a mobile hotel, attached to service trains for the 2,300-mile (3,700 km) itinerary.

THROUGH THE WINDOW

Looking out of the window has always been one of the great pleasures of train travel – except in some modern trains where designers haven't even managed to align seats with windows. To answer the questions that might occur to those of a curious mind regarding the scene passing by, in 1924 the Great Western Railway inaugurated a series called 'Through the Window', beginning with its most scenic main line, from Paddington to Penzance. A mile-by-mile commentary on the landscape and features of interest was provided on the left-hand page and a map of the corresponding section of line on the right. The second volume, *Paddington to Birkenhead*, appeared the following year and *Paddington to Killarney* (via Fishguard) in 1926.

In 1937 the Southern Railway published *A.C.E.: the Atlantic Coast*

Express by S.P.B. Mais (see page 232), which did the same thing for the train from London Waterloo to Ilfracombe, Torrington, Bude, Padstow and Plymouth. It had the added sophistication of red print for places on one side of the train and blue for the other.

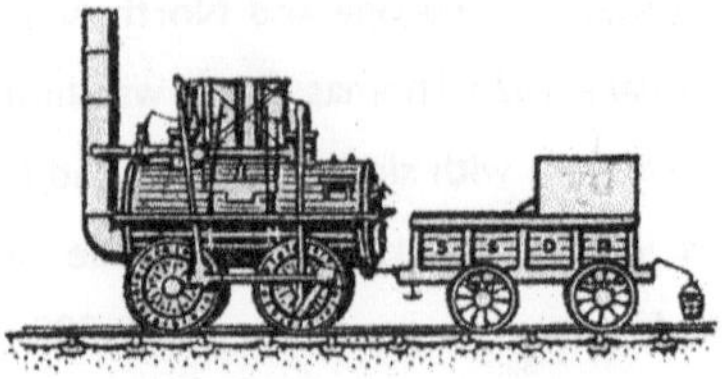

'I'M ON THE TRAIN'

His Highness the Rana of Dholpur didn't want people to be deprived of the knowledge of his presence during the night, so the 12-wheel saloon carriage he had built in 1916 at the Matunga Works of the Great Indian Peninsula Railway had an electrically illuminated coat of arms on the side. The magnificent 68 ft (21 m) long vehicle was finished in cream enamel with blue and gold lining and included a drawing-room, dining-room and kitchen and bedroom with adjacent bathroom.

AFRICAN LUXURY

Cecil Rhodes introduced the 'Zambesi Express de Luxe' in 1902 between Cape Town and Bulawayo. Its 12 bogie carriages included a buffet car with a library and reading-room, a writing-room, card-room, smoking-room and an observation balcony.

MOUNTAINS OF LUGGAGE

It is obvious from paintings of Victorian railway stations that people had not yet learned the art of travelling light. The 1859 *Official Guide to the London & North Western Railway* advised passengers to 'take as little luggage as possible; and ladies are earnestly entreated not to indulge in *more* than seven boxes and five small parcels for the longest journey.' One reason for the greater volumes – apart from the impossibility of being seen in the same dress more than once – was that the well-to-do used to stay longer, whether on holiday in hotels or visiting friends. When Noël Coward set off for the Far East in 1929, he took 27 pieces of luggage and a gramophone.

WHERE'S MY MONKEY?

Left luggage offices have often been the recipients of the strangest objects, only a small proportion of which are ever claimed. Among the items handed in to the London & North Eastern Railway in 1946 was a performing dog which persisted in walking on its hind legs the whole time and following the attendant around, a monkey, a Japanese beheading sword and artificial limbs.

TWENTIETH-CENTURY HORSE POWER

Even in 1914 the horse-drawn Port Carlisle Dandy was an anomaly. This passenger service from Carlisle had begun in 1863 over part of an 11-mile (18 km) railway which was itself a strange affair. It had been built by converting the canal from the 'Border City' to the Solway Firth at Port Carlisle into a standard-gauge railway. The result was a rather dull, flat line that ran in cuttings for much of its length with sudden steep gradients where locks had once been. It opened with steam power in 1854, but two years later a new branch was opened on to Silloth, and it was felt that the sparse traffic on the short section between the junction at Drumburgh and Port Carlisle no longer justified use of a locomotive. A horse was bought for £35 and in the first quarter of 1858 it was estimated that this industrious animal had saved 1,887 engine miles (3,036 km). The following year a purpose-built horse-drawn carriage arrived, Dandy No. 1. First- and second-class passengers were accommodated inside, while third-class passengers perched outside with their backs against the side and their feet resting on footboards.

By 1899 the track had deteriorated to the point where the occasional locomotive-hauled goods service was no longer safe, so even that reverted to horse power. When the decision was taken to end the horse-drawn passenger service on 4 April 1914, picture postcards and a three-verse poem were produced to commemorate the event. No. 1 found a new use as a pavilion at the local bowling club before being rescued by the London & North Eastern Railway for the centenary celebrations of the Stockton & Darlington Railway in 1925. The vehicle then went on display at Edinburgh Waverley and Carlisle Citadel before going to the National Railway Museum in York.

ANIMALS BY TRAIN

The carriage of animals in passenger vehicles led to some curious tickets. The Congo Ocean Railway issued a combined ticket for a dog and monkey, while the Assam Bengal Railway 'small animal' ticket stated that it 'will convey one calf, goat, sheep, pig or other small animal as defined in A.B. Railways Coaching tariff, Para. 201'.

STOPPING FOR A BARBECUE

A relaxed approach to timekeeping characterised some railways on which few trains ran. An example was Mozambique's Beira Railway in its early days as a ramshackle 2 ft gauge operation, to judge from an account by an intrepid lady travelling in December 1895. There were only 10 people in the carriage when Edith Campbell's train left Beira. It slowed so that hunters could shoot at herds of game and stopped when 'Mr Jansen shot a Hartebeeste, cut it up and put it on the train'. At the next passing loop, they were told that there would be a wait of at least an hour to cross a train coming in the other direction, 'so a fire was lit, steaks were cooked, and we picnicked under a big tree. After beer and canned pears for dessert we went on again through lovely forest.' After the train derailed, without inflicting any injuries, they had to wait all night for rescue. In the morning, a man on a trolley arrived 'with a basket of meat, some gin and beer' to keep them going while another engine was rustled up.

CHAPTER SIX

MISHAPS AND SHARP PRACTICE

RAILWAYS HAVE given ample scope for all manner of incidents and escapades, despite the strict discipline of an industry that depends on rules and regulation for its safe operation. Some of these range from the farcical to the extraordinary.

A SOMERSET MISUNDERSTANDING

From 1840, it was the practice for an Inspecting Officer of Railways, drawn from the ranks of the Corps of Royal Engineers, to investigate accidents and make recommendations that would help prevent a similar incident. This highly successful arrangement came to end in 1990 when Her Majesty's Railway Inspectorate became part of the Health and Safety Executive. In 2006 it was transferred to the Office of Rail Regulation, and it finally ceased to exist in 2009 when it was renamed the Safety Directorate. Reports by inspecting officers have provided railway historians with invaluable information and, occasionally, entertainment. Probably the best book on railway accidents is *Red for Danger*, written by that doyen of writers on railways and canals, L.T.C. Rolt. It would be impossible to improve upon his account of one of the most farcical mishaps to occur on Britain's railways.

'Colonel Woodhouse's report on an accident on the Somerset & Dorset Joint Railway on August 4th, 1936, tells a story which, for sheer knockabout comedy, stands unsurpassed in the sober and generally sombre annals of the Railways Inspection Department. The comic element in railway accidents is too often overlaid by tragedy, but in this case there was happily no personal injury whatever.

'The six-coupled side tank engine No. 7620 had been carrying out some shunting operations at Braysdown colliery sidings between Radstock and Wellow and was standing on the up main line, facing south, at the head of eight empty wagons. Her driver became somewhat concerned when he saw bearing down upon him the 9.50am up freight from Evercreech Junction to Bath. It was a heavy train consisting of thirty-seven wagons drawn by one of the massive eight-coupled goods engines built specially by the Midland Company at Derby for work over this steeply graded line. The goods was obviously overrunning signals and the concern of the driver of the shunting tank not unnaturally quickened to alarm when he saw the crew of the big engine leap off the footplate. He immediately flung his engine into back gear, and opened his regulator wide with the object of beating a hasty retreat. By the time he had done this the two engines were practically buffer to buffer and he realised that the goods was now moving very slowly. Quick as thought he jumped out of his cab, clambered on to the footplate of the 2–8–0 and brought her to a stand. Here indeed was cause for self-congratulation! What presence of mind and resource in emergency! How chagrined her craven crew who had so prematurely abandoned ship! But alas, never had pride so speedy a fall. For as our hero had leaped from one side of the footplate, his fireman, a nervous youth, misunderstanding his motive for so doing, had jumped off the other side, and neither had closed the regulator. Triumph instantly turned to dismay when the intrepid driver looked up just in time to see his own engine rapidly disappearing backwards in the direction of Bath propelling the eight wagons before it.

'Fortunately, it was possible to keep the line clear for the runaways.

A few minutes later they roared through Wellow at high speed – 50 miles an hour according to the signalman there. It must have been an alarming sight for him but not one to be compared with the experience of his colleague at Midford, the next station. For here the double line becomes single and the eight wagons proceeded to run well and truly amok on the points and to play havoc with the station and its surroundings. Signals and telegraph poles fell like ninepins; signalman Larcombe's cabin collapsed under his feet as one wagon demolished its masonry base; six wagons shot one after another over an embankment, and for a distance of 300 yards the line was littered with debris. Yet although the track was damaged, No. 7620 held the rails and her powers were by no means exhausted. Having so successfully shaken off most of her load she continued at unabated speed, pushing before her like a handcart the remnant of one wagon running on two wheels only. Miraculously she succeeded in propelling this peculiar vehicle through Combe Down and Devonshire single line tunnels, but Claude Avenue overbridge brought about her undoing. The remaining end door of the wagon fell off, got under her rear wheels and derailed her. At about the same time the fusible plug in the crown of her firebox melted owing to shortage of water and her last breath was spent. The escapade was over.'

WIND GAUGES

It is well known that the worst disaster caused by high wind on a British railway was the destruction of the first Tay Bridge near Dundee during a ferocious storm on the night of 28 December 1879, when all 13 of the high girders crashed into the sea, taking a train and its 78 crew and passengers with them. Though inadequate allowance for wind was compounded by poor workmanship in this case, it encouraged engineers to pay greater attention to the impact of wind on structures. Wind gauges were placed at various places on railway and tram lines, such as Staithes on the Yorkshire coast and Penrhyn Bay on the Llandudno & Colwyn Bay Railway. One was also installed in 1921 on the Halifax Corporation Tramways system near Catherine Slack after two trams were blown over on a wild part of the Pennine moors.

MONSIEUR LE PRESIDENT?

Shortly before midnight on 23 May 1920 the platelayer André Radeau was inspecting newly replaced track between Mignères-Gondreville and Cormy-Corbeille near Orléans when he was approached by a bleeding, bruised and barefoot character dressed in embroidered pyjamas. When the figure announced that he was 'le Président de la République', Radeau thought the man must be drunk or an escapee from a lunatic asylum and led him to a level-crossing house where the *garde-barrière* Gustave Dariot and his wife put him to bed and called the doctor. The doctor recognised the man as the President, M. Paul Deschanel. It transpired that the President, while travelling on an overnight train, had not been feeling well and had been given a sleeping draught of Trional. It had not done the trick and the President was leaning out of a drop-down carriage window when he lost his balance and fell out, mercifully into sand from the new repairs, and while the train was travelling at only 17 mph (30 kph). The incident was a gift to political cartoonists and writers of satirical cabaret songs.

SMELLING A RAT

One of the irritations of crossing European frontiers by train before borders were allowed to become so porous was the need to leave the train, so that customs officials could thoroughly examine the carriages. It was a ploy of smuggling operations for a lady to travel in a train de luxe and insist that she was sick and could not leave her bed. This worked until one day persistent officials were having none of it and found the bed to be stuffed with lace and jewellery.

PITFALLS OF THE FIRST CARRIAGE

Before railways became the safest form of land transport, passengers would often avoid the carriage directly behind the locomotive for fear of an accident. A less commonly known hazard was getting wet, especially in summer when windows and ventilators were open. Among innumerable British railway inventions was the water trough, laid centrally between the rails on a long, dead-flat stretch of track. A scoop beneath the locomotive tender would be quickly lowered into the trough just after the beginning of the trough and hastily wound up before the end. Frequently the fireman, whose job it was to operate the scoop, failed to wind it up in time to stop the tender water tank from overflowing and a deluge would pour on to the leading carriage.

A sad illustration of the damage that could be caused by an overflowing tender occurred on 8 October 1937. Two expresses were passing on Wiske Moor troughs to the north of Northallerton, both hauled by A4 Pacifics. The fireman on the northbound train hauled by No. 4491 *Commonwealth of Australia* lowered the scoop further than he should have and could not lift it. The overflowing water caused considerable damage to the southbound train: 27 carriage ventilator vanes were knocked off and 57 others bent, and two sliding window shutters were broken. But the worst consequence was the shattering of the cab spectacle glass on the southbound locomotive No. 4492 *Dominion of New Zealand*. Tragically, an inspector travelling on the footplate, Charles Skinner, was struck by a piece of glass and collapsed. The signalman at Castle Hills box arranged for an ambulance to be waiting at Northallerton, but Skinner died of 'brain laceration caused by depressed fracture of the skull'.

AN IRISH CONUNDRUM

The Listowel & Ballybunion Railway was one of the few lines built as a monorail. This caused huge difficulties when trying to balance loads in freight wagons. To move a piano, two calves were borrowed, so that one calf could be placed on each side for the return journey. But when a farmer borrowed a cow in Listowel to balance one he had just bought at market, the railway got itself into a frightful pickle, borrowing a second animal to balance the first one borrowed. By the end of the day the farmer had lost his own cow, gained two he didn't want and racked up a tidy sum in freight charges.

RAIL VERSUS AIR

When the RAF aerodrome at Ballykelly in County Londonderry was built in 1941, the runway was designed for light bombers. The decision to base heavier aircraft there entailed extending the runway across the main line from Belfast to Londonderry on the level. Naturally this required a direct link between the control tower and a signal box at the intersection. This was a busy line, and though the trains ran to a schedule, bombers returning from a mission do not. On at least one occasion after peace had returned, a train had to brake violently and an aircraft abort its landing as driver and pilot realised a control tower operative was asleep on the job. The last plane to fly from Ballykelly was a Shackleton in 1971.

ZEPPELIN ARTEFACTS

During the First World War the government gave the London & North Western Railway aluminium from a shot-down Zeppelin to be made into pipe racks, shoe lifts, ashtrays, penholders and other items to raise money for LNWR staff who had joined the Forces.

WORCESTERSHIRE EPITAPH

When steam locomotives were in their infancy, boiler explosions were not uncommon, with fatal results for the footplate crew. One of the earliest was on 10 November 1840 at or near Bromsgrove station at the foot of the famous incline up the Lickey Hills in Worcestershire. The tombstone of one of those killed, Thomas Scaife, was erected by his fellow workmen and bears a poem which must be one of the earliest to use metaphors derived from the component parts of the steam locomotive:

My engine now is cold and still,
No water does my boiler fill,
My coke affords its flame no more,
My days of usefulness are o'er.
My wheels deny their noted speed,
No more my guiding hands they heed,
My whistle, too, has lost its tone,
Its shrill and thrilling sounds are gone.
My valves are now thrown open wide,
My flanges all refuse to guide,
My clacks also, tho' once so strong,
Refuse to aid the busy throng.
No more I feel each urging breath,
My steam is now condens'd in death.
Life's railway's o'er, each station past,
In death I'm stopp'd and rest at last.
Farewell, dear friends, and cease to weep,
In Christ I'm safe, in Him I sleep.

BETTER LATE THAN NEVER

By any standards a train arrival seven years late is extreme. But that is what happened to the 11.30am from Beaumont in Texas to Port Bolivar, a distance of 70 miles (113 km), after its departure on 8 September 1900. It covered the first 33 miles (53 km) to High Island on time, but within a few minutes the train was inundated by the waters of the Gulf of Mexico, which had flooded inland for 40 miles (64 km). The passengers and crew managed to escape after a few hours, leaving the locomotive and four carriages to their fate. When the waters receded, it was discovered that little remained of the railway except for the train and the stretch of track on which it stood. It was seven years before rails were relaid to the site. Astonishingly, after an on-site overhaul, the locomotive was lit up and continued the long-delayed journey, arriving at Port Bolivar to be welcomed by some of its original passengers.

LEVEL-CROSSING FRACAS

The story nominated by an insurance group as the most bizarre rental car accident of 1999 took place around a level crossing somewhere in the East Midlands. A driver approaching the crossing, which was closed, slammed on his brakes when he saw a horse and a pensioner walking his dog. A motorcyclist behind him bumped into the car and was thrown over it, landing behind the horse and scaring it so much that it reared up and threw the rider into a hawthorn hedge. While the horse bolted up the road, the pensioner went to help the horse-rider, first tying his Yorkshire Terrier to the nearest object, the level-crossing barrier. As the train passed the crossing, the barrier rose, so the dog's owner rushed to rescue the choking animal from the barrier. Agitated and confused, the dog expressed its gratitude by sinking its teeth into the prostrate motorcyclist.

FOUR-LEGGED FRIENDS

Another collecting dog, London Jack, is preserved, on the Bluebell Railway in Sussex. London Jack spent much of his life at Waterloo raising £4,500 for the Southern Railway orphanage at Woking, where that institution's successor still receives funds raised today by Jack. Other collecting dogs were Nell at Bournemouth, Prince at Croydon, Gyp at Southampton and Bernie at Waterloo. The champion collector seems to have been Sandy, who extracted £9,000 from passengers at Exeter Central between 1944 and 1952, while the laziest was Twister at Merthyr, who used to lie down as soon as the collecting box was strapped on to him.

LIGHT FINGERS

Railways have proved a tempting target for thieves from the very start. The Liverpool & Manchester Railway, the world's first 'modern' railway, opened in 1830 and the following year the theft of oranges and oysters during passage through tunnels was reported. Some suspicion was falling on staff, who were caught illegally carrying letters on their own account and were certainly pilfering candles from the works – the LMR resorted to having coloured candles made which could be easily identified if taken off the premises.

BREACH OF TRUST

White-collar crime has been a rarity on Britain's railways, thanks in part to systems developed after one of the most spectacular deceptions of Victorian times. During the 1840s a young clerk named Leopold Redpath found himself in charge of the share registration department of the Great Northern Railway. He had been promoted on the recommendation of the company's leaving Secretary, but not even the most basic checks had been made about Redpath's past when he was first taken on by the GNR. Had they been done, it would have been revealed that Redpath was a declared bankrupt and that he had left his previous employment with the London & Brighton Railway under a cloud.

Redpath devised a scheme whereby he would create new stock – for example by inserting an extra digit on stock transfers and forging names – which he would then sell through brokers to ordinary investors. Naturally the company was paying out dividends on a steadily rising amount of issued stock for which it had received no capital. Alarm bells about the discrepancy began ringing in February 1854, but it was not until October 1856 that the process behind the fraud was discovered, whereupon Redpath fled to Paris. During the eight years that Redpath went undetected, he had deprived the

GNR of £240,000. Redpath decided to return to face the music and was tried at the Central Criminal Court in January 1857. He became one of the last people to be sentenced to transportation for life, dying in Sydney in 1891.

Following the revelations, the GNR called in W.W. Deloitte, who in 1845 had opened up an office in Basinghall Street, London, becoming in 1849 the very first person to be appointed as an independent auditor when he was given the task by the Great Western Railway. Over the following two decades he was responsible for developing railway accounting systems that extinguished opportunities for would-be Redpaths.

JUST NOT CRICKET

On the eve of a cricket match between two Yorkshire villages, underhand measures were taken at a station on the East Riding line between Malton and Driffield, where the clerk was an outstanding spin bowler. The opposing team was so worried about his prowess and the thought of defeat that, when they discovered he had to catch the last train of the day to get to the match, they devised a subterfuge. As many of the villagers as could be spared would go to the station two or three minutes before the last train was due, to make spurious enquiries about missing parcels or request times for complicated train journeys. They succeeded in making the poor man miss his train and the match.

DECEIT AND DECEPTION

There were few railwaymen in the 1960s and '70s who could not cite instances of British Railways deliberately undermining the economic case for retaining a railway line it wanted to close: costs were inflated by unnecessary expenditure, timetables altered so that connections were deliberately missed, and little effort was made at intelligent modernisation of operations to reduce overheads.

Astonishingly, the railway unions never marshalled this evidence to mount a robust defence of the industry and oppose closures, many of which are now regarded as a mistake. Nor did the Transport Users' Consultative Committees scrutinise many closure proposals with a sufficiently critical eye. To make matters worse, governments of neither persuasion had the prescience to insist on the integrity of the trackbed being maintained, so that lines could be reopened.

Having succeeded in fobbing off local communities with a second-rate bus replacement, which itself would be withdrawn within a year or two, British Railways often lost no time making quite sure the closure was irreversible. Demolition gangs moved in immediately; the largest single closure to date was enacted at midnight on 28 February 1959, with the closure of 156 miles (251 km) of the Midland & Great

IT'S GOOD TO TALK

When the Réseau Breton branch from Paimpol to Guingamp in Brittany was converted from metre gauge to standard, gangs started at each end of the line. But they evidently did not talk to each other, as they chose different sides of the track to lay the third rail . . .

Northern Joint main line across Lincolnshire and Norfolk. A signalman who had worked Sutton Bridge signal-box for 39 years watched its destruction within hours of his last shift, and it was announced to the Press that hastily recovered signalling equipment was urgently required elsewhere.

CONFISCATING LOCOMOTIVES

Rivalry between railway companies in the 19th century was as territorial as the animal kingdom. Extreme measures were taken to keep competitors out of towns and cities that companies regarded as 'theirs'. Usually this entailed spoiling tactics such as opposing Bills in Parliament, buying up minor lines and promoting rival schemes. Sometimes things got more exciting.

In 1849 the East Lancashire Railway and the Lancashire & Yorkshire Railway were at loggerheads over tolls paid per passenger by the ELR for journeys between Clifton Junction station and Salford, a section owned by the LYR. The ELR had decided to run some trains that did not serve Clifton station and would declare the number being carried, but the LYR demanded they stop so that the numbers could be checked. A LYR threat to blockade the line was countered by an injunction, but at 10.30am on 12 March a gang of LYR workmen tied a baulk across the rails and a train of six empty carriages with a locomotive at the Salford end was placed in the platform blocking the ELR train's route. Police were present and the baulk was removed. The ELR train then tried to push the LYR train forward, without success. The counterattack came in the form of an ELR stone train to block LYR trains. By midday eight trains were backed up on each side of the obstructions, and the delayed passengers were remonstrating with railway staff. The stand-off was ended by the LYR removing their train first.

Three years later it was the Midland and Great Northern railways at loggerheads over London–Nottingham services. The GNR had entered into an agreement with the independent Ambergate, Nottingham & Boston & Eastern Junction Railway to operate trains over the line between Grantham and Colwick from where there were running rights into the Midland's station in Nottingham. This approach from Grantham would make GNR trains from London faster than the Midland's via Derby. The MR obtained an injunction preventing the GNR operating this line, so when the first GNR service arrived in Nottingham from King's Cross, the Midland felt justified in trapping the 'intruding' locomotive with its own engines. The hapless GNR crew were evicted, the locomotive was locked in a shed and the rails to it were removed. There it remained for the next seven months. After much legal wrangling, the GNR took over the independent company on a lease optimistically running until the year 2854 and built its own station in Nottingham at London Road.

In 1858 a dispute arose between the London & South Western and the London Brighton & South Coast railways over running powers between Havant and Portcreek Junction. The LSWR had decided to operate a privately built line between Godalming and Havant which possessed such running rights; it was announced that passenger services would begin on New Year's Day 1859. To test the water, a goods train was run on 28 December, and the LSWR clearly anticipated trouble over the few miles of LBSCR-owned track to Portcreek Junction to reach the joint LSWR/LBSCR line into Portsmouth. Aboard the 'goods train' were about 80 platelayers and other 'rough and ready employees' of the LSWR, together with a barrel of beer and other provisions. On arrival at Havant they found that the points had been disconnected and a Brighton locomotive placed on the crossing. The platelayers quickly relaid the point and seized the Brighton engine. Expecting retaliation, they lifted a rail on the Brighton line and placed the goods train on the crossing, blocking both lines. When a rival force arrived, it looked as though a fight would ensue, but the traffic manager of the LSWR exercised prudence and retreated to Guildford, leaving the next move to the lawyers. An injunction was obtained restraining the LBSCR, and through trains to Portsmouth began on 24 January.

OFF THE RAILS

An accident in 1831 at Huyton Colliery on the Liverpool & Manchester Railway was caused by the wind blowing a wagon of coal into the path of a passenger train. Many wagons were unbraked at the time, and evidently no one had the wit to place a chock under the wheels.

AN IRISH FARCE

Rather different was the seizure of an entire train for debt on the Athenry & Ennis Junction Railway in the counties of Galway and Clare. On 10 November 1870, the County Clare sheriff impounded a train of clapped-out rolling stock and would only allow it to depart with a posse of bailiffs on the footplate. The County Galway sheriff thought it time he got in on the act and a few days later Galway officers tried to evict the Clare men from the footplate. The passengers looked on while the forces of law indulged in a bout of fisticuffs, with the Galway officers triumphant.

When it came to making something out of this contretemps, it was discovered that the locomotive – the only thing of any value – was still owned by a finance company, which put it on the market. The engine's condition was so deplorable that there was only one bidder – the Athenry & Ennis Junction Railway.

A ROYAL SIGNAL

Extreme measures sometimes had to be taken with royal trains. When Queen Elizabeth and Prince Philip were returning from Sandringham to London Liverpool Street one day, a signal arm protecting the approach to the terminus parted from the cast-iron spectacle casing and fell to the ground. There was no time to implement normal safety procedures without delaying the train, so a porter was sent up the signal to hold the arm in place until the royal train had passed.

LULLED TO SLEEP

Driving goods trains called for considerable skill in steam days. Only fast goods trains had wagons with brakes that could be applied from the locomotive, and link rather than screw couplings meant that the slack in the couplings had to be taken up gently; if it wasn't, the poor guard at the end of a long train could be knocked off his feet by the accumulated jolting. It also ran the risk of breaking a coupling.

This is what happened early one morning on the West Highland line when a northbound goods train off Glasgow at 2.15am accelerated too hastily away from Corrour, having slowed to collect the single-line tablet for the next section to Tulloch. The coupling between the brake van and the rest of the train broke, but the guard was fast asleep. Most of the train was over the summit but the brake van was not, so having come to a halt it began to return whence it came. The Corrour signalman alerted his counterpart at Rannoch of the runaway, presenting an unenviable dilemma: the Rule Book required him to derail the brake van, but when he saw the speed it was going he knew that action would condemn the somnolent guard to injury or death. With no other northbound train due for some time, he allowed the brake van to rattle through the station.

The signalman at Gorton had the same reaction and estimated it was doing about 35 mph (56 kph) as it swept past on the long descent to Bridge of Orchy. There, the stationmaster estimated that if the brake van survived the curves en route, the gently rising gradient beyond the station would arrest its progress. He therefore followed the van on foot and caught up with it about 2 miles (3.2 km) to the south. Having shaken the guard awake, the stationmaster asked him if he knew where he was. When told he was at Bridge of Orchy, the guard protested, 'Ach, don't be daft, we were there two hours ago.'

'Well, you're back there again,' replied the stationmaster.

OFF THE RAILS

Passengers aboard a French TGV from Paris to La Rochelle on Monday 27 October 2008 were delayed for about two hours by a man who had his arm stuck down a toilet. The 26-year-old passenger's arm got trapped up to the shoulder by the vacuum flushing system after he accidentally dropped his mobile phone into the loo and tried to retrieve it. Emergency workers took more than an hour to cut him free, carrying him from the train on a stretcher with the toilet still stuck to his arm. A fire department spokesman said: 'He was cut free from the toilet on the platform, and apart from suffering bruising and smelling a bit he suffered no other injuries.' But he had missed a number of calls.

LANDSLIP AT FOLKESTONE WARREN

One of the most costly stretches of track to maintain has been between Folkestone and Dover, an area of soft chalk resting on barely permeable blue clay where the North Downs meet the sea. The warren is approached from Folkestone through the 1,596 ft (486 m) Martello Tunnel, and it was near here that the worst of many landslips took place, on 19 December 1915. A railway watchman heard a rumbling sound from near the eastern end of the tunnel at about 6.30pm. Knowing an Ashford–Dover train was due, he summoned help from soldiers at a sentry post near the shore and they tied red flags around oil lamps and bravely walked along the sinking railway towards the tunnel. The driver saw the red lights before emerging from the tunnel, but the train was outside it by the time he could bring it to a halt. The 130 passengers on board were soon aware of the reason, as the carriages creaked and moved with the sliding ground. The passengers were escorted back through the tunnel to Folkestone Junction station, without injury. The scene in the morning was bizarre. The train was largely still on the track but it resembled a dip in a fairground rollercoaster, and the magnitude of the movements had raised the seabed, creating a lagoon.

Railwaymen further east had an equally lucky escape. The signalman at Abbots Cliff signal-box had been alerted by a platelayer who dashed into the box to tell him to halt all trains. Minutes later the track worker returned to tell the signalman to quit the box quickly as the cliff was moving and the two men ran for safety away from the hillside. Within moments the signal-box was swept away. The damage along the coast was so severe that the railway remained closed for the rest of the First World War, and only reopened on 11 August 1919.

CHAPTER SEVEN

SPECIAL TRAINS

THE TERM 'special trains' is used in this chapter to encompass trains run not only for special occasions but also for specialised commodities, which might be operated on a regular basis. The greatest obstacle to railways carrying such traffic has been the companies' ever stricter accounting practices, under which traffic using rolling stock on a sporadic basis is deemed uneconomic, even though the cost of that stock may have been completely written off through depreciation. So the days of being able to rustle up a set of carriages at short notice, or to supply wagons for a sudden spike in demand, are largely past. In some countries the provision of excursion trains, previously the role of state or national companies, has been taken over by private organisations.

GNR

THE CANADIAN SILK TRAINS

No train had higher priority in train schedules across Canada than the silk trains which from the 1880s carried Japanese raw silk from the port of Vancouver to the mills of New York and New Jersey for turning into stockings. Armed guards travelled with these crack trains to protect a cargo that could be worth up to $2 million. Because the silk was perishable, it had to reach its destination as quickly as possible. The longshoremen in Vancouver prided themselves on loading a 30-tonne boxcar in 15 minutes, and customs inspections were kept to a minimum. The silk trains often reached 90 mph (145 kph), overtaking even the top passenger trains, and could arrive in New York from Vancouver in 97 hours. A fireman working out of Revelstoke described them as 'the fastest and most hair-raising runs I ever made'. The trains died out with the replacement of the silk stocking by nylon following the Second World War.

CATTLE CLASS

The term is used today to describe overcrowded trains or cramped planes, but in the case of the South Staffordshire Railway, in 1849, it became rather too true when a shortage of rolling stock compelled the use of cattle trucks. Young tykes beside the line took to 'mooing' at the passengers as they passed, and the experiment was not repeated.

THE NORTHERN BELLE

This cruise train was inaugurated by the London & North Eastern Railway in 1933 and ran until 1939. For an inclusive fare of £20, up to 60 first-class passengers enjoyed a week's 2,000-mile (3,200 km) sightseeing holiday punctuated by coach and lake steamer excursions. Besides the air-conditioned sleeping cars whose cabins had shower baths fed by 100-gallon tanks mounted on the underframe, there were carriages with lounge, writing-room, shop, hairdressing salon and ladies' retiring-room. The 27 travelling staff had their own quarters, bringing the number of carriages to 15.

CHARTERS FOR DEMONSTRATIONS

Until the advent of the motor coach, the railways were the only means by which protestors could assemble for national demonstrations. The frequency and number of special trains for all manner of events enabled the railways to maintain thousands of carriages for the purpose. A measure of the demand for extra trains is provided by the demonstrations in London in 1912 against the Disestablishment of the Welsh Episcopal Church, which required 32 special trains from Wales, run by the Great Western and London & North Western railways.

THE FIRST EXCURSION

It is often claimed that the first excursion train was a temperance outing from Leicester to Loughborough in July 1841 organised by Thomas Cook. In fact, such trains are almost as old as the railway, for on the day after the opening of the Liverpool & Manchester Railway on 15 September 1830, the Society of Friends chartered a train to take 130 members from Liverpool to Manchester for a meeting. However, because they paid the standard first-class fare of 7 shillings (35p) each way, some railway historians refuse to allow it excursion status, since a characteristic of the excursion train is a reduction on the normal fare. So perhaps the credit must go to the Canterbury & Whitstable Railway, which ran a train with a reduced fare on 19 March 1832.

Another contender is the Bodmin & Wenford Railway, which packed 800 people into two trains of open wagons in June 1836, taking excursionists from Wadebridge to Wenford Bridge. The event that made the excursion part of British national life was the Great Exhibition of 1851, when many of the six million visitors travelled by train for the first time, 165,000 of them on Cook-organised excursions. Thomas Hardy, in his short story 'The Fiddler of the Reels', described the appearance of those aboard open wagons on an excursion arriving at Waterloo from Wessex for the Great Exhibition: 'blue-faced, stiff-necked, sneezing, rain-beaten, chilled to the marrow, many of the men being hatless; in fact, they resembled people who had been out all night on a rough sea, rather than inland excursionists for pleasure.'

A DAY AT THE RACES

Race traffic quickly became a staple business of the railway, the first instance being in 1838 when special trains were run from Nine Elms, on London's south bank, to Kingston, then the nearest station for Epsom races. So many people turned up to travel that the inexperienced railway couldn't cope and had to suspend services. The revenue potential encouraged construction of special stations to serve such racecourses as Newbury, Cheltenham, Wetherby and Lanark where a main station was too distant from the course. In 1883 a station was even built on the freight-only ironstone branch to Waltham-on-the-Wolds in Leicestershire, for Croxton Park races.

One of the busiest events of the racing calendar was St Leger Day at Doncaster. So many trains had to be handled that every siding was cleared and even temporary signal-boxes were created to increase line capacity on the approaches. In 1887, Doncaster saw the arrival of 82 special trains, which had to be marshalled in sidings so at the end of racing a train could depart in precise sequence every 75 seconds from 5.45pm to 7.30pm.

On Grand National day in 1913, Aintree station received 91 trains in addition to a shuttle of electric trains on the Liverpool Overhead Railway, which between them delivered 34,000 people.

CHOCOLATE TRAINS

In the 20th century companies saw the public relations value of visits to their factories. As in Switzerland today, chocolate factories proved popular destinations, and in 1938 excursion trains brought 71,455 to Keynsham station for a visit to Fry's Somerdale factory near Bristol. Cadbury Bros of Bournville and Terry's of York also welcomed excursionists.

OH! I DO LIKE TO BE BESIDE THE SEASIDE

Sea air and the pleasures of coastal resorts proved probably the richest vein for railway excursions. In the days before foreign travel was thinkable for more than a small part of the population, coastal resorts saw prodigious influxes of visitors during the summer. Mablethorpe on the Lincolnshire coast had a permanent population of about 930 in 1913, but during the three months of July, August and September this was increased by 28,000 overnight visitors, as well as a far greater number of day and half-day 'excursionists'.

What is most extraordinary about some early sea-bound excursion trains is their prodigious size. On 8 April 1844, for example, an excursion of 60 carriages hauled by six locomotives steamed into Brighton on the London & Brighton Railway. Even allowing for the small four-wheeled carriages of the day, such a train could never have been accommodated at a platform, so it must either have performed lengthy shunting manoeuvres or disgorged its passengers without the use of a platform.

CHEAP TRIP FOR FEMALES

An excursion handbill from 1849 targeted 'females' who had wanted to join a previous excursion from Maudland station to Fleetwood on the Lancashire coast. They and children were offered tickets at half the price charged to men. It was operated on 6 August 1849 just after the Lancashire & Yorkshire and London & North Western railways had jointly taken over the ailing Preston & Wyre Railway. The Victorian faith in the restorative properties of sea air are indicated by the suggestion that 'employers . . . who do not arrange for trips on their own account, may avail themselves of this opportunity of sending down any of the sick or other hands whom they may be desirous of treating. A steamer will ply through the day to take persons round the Light-house at 2d each.' A section entitled 'Advice' contains some obvious points about arriving in good time and looking after your ticket but also this admonition: 'Above all things show an accommodating disposition, and a wish to oblige; this will materially assist in making the excursion pleasant.'

The excursionists visiting Fleetwood for the first time might well have been alarmed by the nature of the approach to the embryonic town, since it was the nearest thing in Britain to the remarkable railway that stretched for 114 miles (183 km) along coral islets to Key West in Florida. For almost 2 miles (3.2 km) the Lancashire line ran partially on a stone-faced embankment and partly on piles, so that it seemed to be crossing an inland sea. Structural problems with the embankment prompted its abandonment following construction of an alternative approach to Fleetwood in 1851.

MILITARY MANOEUVRES

Exercises for militias and the Territorials were a common feature of the summer months before the First World War. In 1911 the forested area around Thetford in Norfolk was the War Office's choice, and the Great Eastern Railway was called upon to provide the logistics. An early harvest that summer prevented many attending the annual training, but the GER still had to move 12,000 men, over 1,100 horses, 50 guns and more than 150 wagons of military equipment as well as tents, bedding and food for men and horses. On one weekend over 400 carriages and wagons had to be dealt with, and the final weekend saw the dispatch of 33 special trains in addition to the normal service trains.

INVALID CARRIAGES

Before the First World War, well-appointed saloon carriages were available for the transport of invalids and their carers, though some were also available for hire as family saloons. To eliminate vibration from the train's motion, the Great Western Railway suspended a couch/bed from the roof with sprung slings.

A HOLIDAY IN KENT

For many families enduring squalid housing in the East End of London, the late August migration to help harvest hops in Kent was the nearest they had to a holiday. Until the second half of the 20th century many Kent landscapes would be covered in hops as far as the eye could see. Paddock Wood was the epicentre of the hop fields, and the first train to it ran in 1844. The South Eastern (later the South Eastern & Chatham) Railway handled most of the traffic, and special rakes of small four-wheel carriages, deemed unfit for normal service, were kept for the 'hoppers'. Regular hop-picking families would be notified by postcard from the farmer with details of date, train time and destination.

Usually about 30,000 people went to work in the fields for several weeks, so luggage vans had to be added to the train, but the men would return to their usual jobs at the end of the weekend, leaving their wives and children to do the work. These specials proved a boon to the impoverished Kent & East Sussex Railway; its station at Bodiam, a place best known for its castle, was situated among hop fields owned by Guinness. But the busiest time for the railway was the intermediate weekends when it ran special trains for 'hop-pickers' friends' who went down for a day visit and could number over 40,000. A Hop-pickers' Friends Special of up to 15 bogie coaches was quite a contrast to the branch line's usual single coach.

The hop-pickers returned towards the end of September, and efforts had to be made to ensure they did not arrive at London Bridge when commuters were making homeward journeys. In 1912 these events were badly timed, resulting in a 'pandemonium of men, women, children, babies and bundles, none of which smelt any too sweet'. This traffic was still sufficiently large in the 1950s for the Southern Region to set up a 'Hop Control' room at Paddock Wood. But a collapse in demand for Kent hops for brewing because of imported beers and hops all but wiped out the industry in the 1960s – the very time when British Railways was getting rid of the excursion stock that carried the hop-pickers.

Freight traffic was not all outbound hops – bulky but light. The best fertiliser for the hops was ammonia- and nitrogen-rich 'shoddy', delivered in vans from the mills of Bradford and Kidderminster (carpets) in particular.

CANADIAN ROYAL TRAINS

On 29 September 1901 a series of photographs was taken at Glacier between Revelstoke and Field on the Canadian Pacific Railway, showing six members of the royal party on the buffer beam of a steam locomotive, wrapped up in travelling rugs. Two of them were the Duke and Duchess of York (from 1910 George V and Queen Mary). They were also recorded as riding through the Fraser Canyon on the buffer beam.

One of the photographers recording the separate trains of the Governor-General and the royal party was Edward Whymper, who 36 years previously had led the first, fateful ascent of the Matterhorn. To make sure they got up the 'Big Hill' from Field without difficulty, five locomotives were used. This was one of the toughest sections of railway to build and operate anywhere in the world. Built in 1884 as a temporary route, it was not replaced until the famous spiral tunnels were completed in 1909. The 8-mile (13 km) section had a gradient of 1 in 22 and sharp curves, requiring eastbound ascending trains to have four, five or even six locomotives at various places in the train to distribute their weight and reduce the strain on couplings.

It was apparently Agnes Macdonald, the second wife of Canada's first Prime Minster Sir John Macdonald, who established a vogue for riding on the front buffer beam. In July 1886 they were travelling across the country together for the first time. Sir John was worn out by the struggle to get the line built and was reclusive, but she announced at Laggan that she wanted to experience the line from the front and had a platform built over a locomotive buffer beam with a chair fixed to it so that she could have an unimpeded view of the railway. Despite her husband's reservations, her will prevailed. How far she travelled in this exhilarating manner does not appear to have been recorded, but she must have been a lady with plenty of chutzpah.

When George VI and Queen Elizabeth visited Canada in 1939, they travelled across the country from Quebec City to Vancouver by train. The steam locomotives rostered to work the train were specially painted in royal blue with silver trim, as was the train. As something of a railway buff, the king rode on the footplate when feasible and afterwards gave permission for the semi-streamlined Canadian Pacific Hudsons (4–6–4 wheel arrangement) to be known as Royal Hudsons and display the royal crown. Two of the royal carriages, the Mount

Stephen and the Royal Wentworth, today form part of the Royal Canadian Pacific charter train.

CHURCHES ON WHEELS

The Russian royal train included a church car, but they were also to be found along the Trans-Siberian Railway, complete with icons, bells and travelling priests. At stations along the way where churches had yet to be built, church cars were used to hold services for local people, railway workers and passengers.

A similar carriage was put into service in the US in 1912 for the Catholic Church Extension Society of the United States of America. The 75 ft (23 m) touring chapel car for missionary use was carried on six-wheel bogies. The chapel was fitted with altar, sanctuary, confessional and organ and accommodated 60. There were also sleeping berths, a dining-room/study, a superintendent's room, shower bath and toilet, and a fully equipped kitchen.

CIRCUS TRAINS

The arrival of the circus train was an eagerly awaited event in the lives of many children, and the procession from station to the site for the big top was stage-managed to extract maximum publicity for the show as well as adhere to tight schedules. Circus trains were sometimes built to order, reflecting their specialised nature, but in 1912 the Great Eastern Railway felt justified in building a common-user elephant van similar to the four-wheeled vans designed to convey prize cattle by passenger train. The loading gauge prevented anything larger than a baby or Indian elephant being carried.

But the longest circus train must have been that of the US impresario Phineas T. Barnum, whose 'Greatest Show on Earth' required a train of 61 vehicles, purpose-built in the 1870s. It carried 1,000 staff, 30 elephants and a big top that seated 5,000. When Barnum came to Europe in 1889 as Barnum & Bailey, he began with a Christmas show at Olympia in London before setting off on a five-year tour using 67 vehicles, which had to be run in three portions. After Barnum's death in 1891, Bailey brought a second grand tour to Europe in 1899, following which the Pullman cars in which the star performers had travelled were sold to the Alexandra Docks Railway, where they ran between Newport and Pontypridd.

TO THE MATCH

Railways made professional football possible. As a game it grew in popularity following the granting of a half-day on Saturday in the 1850 Ten

Hour Act, and within half a century there were about 200 professional clubs and thousands of amateur teams.

Hooliganism on trains had reared its ugly head by 1892, when damage was caused to a train returning from Cambridge with Oxford University students. The London & North Western Railway was later reimbursed and a donation was made to the Railway Benevolent Fund.

Better behaviour was obviously expected of Grimsby Town supporters in 1911 when the *Grimsby Telegraph* chartered a luncheon-car special from the Great Central Railway for the Grimsby v. Nottingham Forest away game. The price of 4s 9d (24p) return included lunch. A reporter was probably not being euphemistic when he wrote that the late return departure time of 11.10pm would give Grimsby supporters plenty of time 'to get over their feelings' after the match.

For the 1931 international between Scotland and England at Hampden Park in Glasgow, 218 special trains were run, helping to create a world record gate for any game of 129,810.

THE SHOW MUST GO ON

Theatre companies were a major source of revenue: on Sunday 22 October 1911, the London & North Western Railway alone moved 112 theatrical companies, carrying 2,374 passengers, 182 scenery trucks and 8 horseboxes, by service trains and 30 specials. One of the specials, from Manchester to Carlisle, carried six different companies.

MAIL TRAINS

The carriage of mail by train prompted one of the finest documentary films made in Britain – John Grierson's 1936 *Night Mail* with the poetry of W.H. Auden and the music of Benjamin Britten. Its subject was the travelling post offices which ran overnight, picking up and dropping off mail at stations and on the move from lineside apparatus, with the mail behind sorted and bagged en route. The idea of picking up mail on the move was a legacy of coaching days, when the horses would be slowed but not stop. The first travelling post office (TPO) was a converted horsebox of the Grand Junction Railway (GJR) running between Birmingham and Warrington in January 1838. Its success prompted an order for four four-wheelers with accommodation for two clerks and four guards.

An apparatus for picking up and dropping off mail bags at speed was designed by the carriage builder Nathaniel Worsdell, who had built the tender for the Stephensons' *Rocket* and supplied carriages to the GJR. He asked the Post Office for £5,000 for the patented device, but they declined and ended up using a receiving net and 'crane' designed by an official in the Missing Letter Branch of the Post Office, John Ramsey.

The apogee of TPOs was in 1938, when 77 overnight services were operated. The West Coast service between London Euston and Aberdeen made 60 exchanges during its run. It was a useful service to be able to post an urgent letter into the postbox on the side of a mail coach, not only in London but at calling points on the way. London sorters would work as far as Carlisle, where they would be relieved by a team taking over for the remainder of the journey to Aberdeen. If a train sorter was still on the rails after a year, they generally stayed for life, and many had over 40 years of service. Many said the hours flew by, as they worked at a pace that allowed no time for clock-watching.

The last use of lineside apparatus was on 4 October 1971 at

Penrith, and the last mail sorting on the move was on the North Eastern TPO between Willesden and Newcastle on the night of 9 January 2004. Mail exchange apparatus has been preserved in working order at Didcot Railway Centre and on the Great Central and Nene Valley railways.

FOUR-LEGGED FRIENDS

For 10 years between 1860 and 1870, a Fox Terrier named Snatchbury used to travel on the footplate of the locomotive on the 5pm London Euston to Holyhead express when its driver was a man named Shelby. The driver was killed at Harrow when he drove a train past a signal at danger in fog on 26 November 1870, but Snatchbury survived and attached himself to another driver for the next five years.

EXCURSIONS FOR RAMBLERS AND CYCLISTS

Both pastimes became extremely popular between the two world wars. Railway companies published books of walks from railway stations and ran hikers' excursion trains, some to 'mystery' destinations. The Great Western Railway was the most prolific publisher, but the Southern published many walking books by S.P.B. Mais (see page 232), such as the

1938 *Let's Get Out Here* suggesting 26 walks from stations at which the 'Atlantic Coast Express' stopped.

In conjunction with the Ramblers' Association, the Southern Region during the 1950s organised Conducted Ramble Trains once a fortnight throughout the year, often taking such interesting railway routes that they also attracted railway enthusiasts.

In May 1938 the Southern Railway ran a special train with five vans to take bikes to Winchester for the New Forest. In British Railways' days, some lines that were closed to passengers but still open for freight were used by ramblers' specials.

PIGEON SPECIALS

Well into the 1960s the operation of pigeon specials for long-distance weekend races was an important sideline to the railway's parcels business. Baskets of birds were taken to a distant point, where the station staff released them, writing the time of release on a label attached to the returning empty basket. The Friday night/Saturday morning roster of racing pigeon specials could be intricate, with remarshalling of vans at junctions. A Dudley–Bath train, for example, might contain vans originating from Lichfield, Walsall, Wolverhampton, Rugeley and Dudley itself. Most of the trains were from north to south, and some even entailed shipping the pigeons from Weymouth or Southampton to northern France. Convoyers in two passenger coaches would accompany the birds in the corridor-connected ventilated bogie vans so that they could be fed and watered. The North Eastern Railway, serving an area where pigeon fancying was particularly popular, made special pigeon vans with shelving arranged to allow maximum ventilation.

One July weekend in 1911, over 1,250 baskets of pigeons were sent from Southampton to St Malo for release from Rennes in Brittany. At an average of a dozen birds per basket, about 15,000 birds would have been released at the French city, a sight which must have aroused some choice remarks among the inhabitants.

A RECORD EVEN FOR BLACKPOOL

It's impossible to say with certainty when Blackpool received the most visitors by train, but 21 June 1919 must be a candidate: a day when the Lancashire & Cheshire Miners' Federation decided to combine a demonstration on the sands with a family day out. The Lancashire & Yorkshire Railway had to cope with 135 trains bringing over 100,000 miners and their families, a train arriving every three or four minutes.

Another huge influx was seen on 20 September 1952, the day of the Blackpool Illuminations. The numbers they carried are not recorded, but Blackpool Central received 113 trains and Blackpool North 126.

EVENING CRUISE TRAINS

Between the world wars, the London Midland & Scottish and London & North Eastern railways operated evening cruise trains around such areas as the southern Highlands, the Borders and the North York Moors. Dining-cars served teas and light refreshments. They proved so popular that some excursions had to run in several portions. To confound the doctrinaire belief that the nationalised British Railways lacked enterprise, the idea was developed after the Second World War into the land cruise train, notably in North Wales.

BY ROYAL APPOINTMENT

The operation of royal trains has caused more headaches than any other type of train, for obvious reasons, though the problems were compounded in Queen Victoria's case by her dislike of what then passed for high speed. This aversion wasn't helped by her physician being killed in a derailment at Raynes Park in 1861. The elaborate security arrangements included the passage of a pilot engine in advance of the royal train and the locking of level-crossing gates at least an hour before the royal train was due.

The larger railway companies in Britain vied to produce ever more opulent carriages for Her Majesty and her entourage. The

OFF THE RAILS

A photograph taken at a station near Port Elizabeth in South Africa, probably in the early 20th century, became a postcard for its curious subject. It showed a uniformed railwayman who had lost both legs below the knee and a baboon which he had trained to pull the levers on an open-air lever frame.

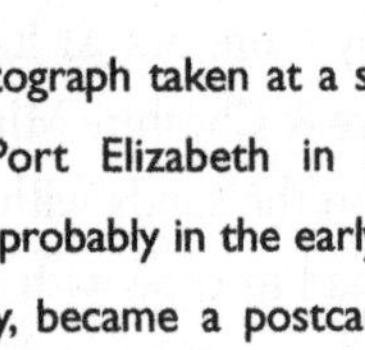

first royal journey by train was on 15 October 1839, when the Dowager Queen Adelaide travelled from London Euston to Rugby for a visit to Lord Denbigh at Newnham Paddox in Warwickshire. In the absence of a royal carriage, a mail coach was hastily sent to the London works of Joseph Wright, who had begun building railway carriages in 1835 at Gough Street, in Clerkenwell, and is credited with building the first carriages for the London & Birmingham Railway. Wright had three days to make the carriage fit for a queen, with trimming of flowered silk, gilded mouldings and a repaint of the carriage. Wright moved his works to Saltley in Birmingham in 1845, the business becoming the famous Metropolitan Carriage & Wagon Works in 1862. Three carriages built by him in the 1850s for the first railway in New South Wales are preserved in the Powerhouse Museum in Sydney.

The first journey by a reigning monarch was on 13 June 1842, when Victoria and Prince Albert entrained at Slough for London Paddington (the Windsor branch was not opened until 1849). Before departure, the Queen's Master of the Horse had inspected the station and train and expressed some misgivings that would almost certainly have been founded in ignorance of the new mode of transport. Brunel and the Great Western Railway's 'Superintendent of Locomotive Engines' Daniel Gooch were on the footplate of the almost new locomotive *Phlegethon.* They were joined by the Queen's coachman, who could not be convinced that Her Majesty would be safe without his presence on the footplate. The next day the Queen wrote to her uncle Leopold, King of the Belgians, that she had come by 'the railroad . . . free from dust and crowd and heat' and that she was 'quite charmed with it'.

The National Railway Museum in York has several royal saloons, including most remarkably the first purpose-built royal carriage, built for Queen Adelaide in, it is thought, 1842.

TO THE FINLAND STATION

One of the most portentous railway journeys ever made was Lenin's return to Russia in 1917, '. . . in a Sealed Train like a plague bacillus from Switzerland to Russia' as Winston Churchill put it. The train left Zürich on 8 April, not without drama. Other Russian exiles were unhappy that Lenin should be helping their country's enemy, Germany, by returning to foment revolution; they besieged Lenin and the 30 exiles travelling with him and implored him not to go. He ignored them, but a moment later he had pitched a suspected stool pigeon out of the compartment on to the platform. They travelled by Swiss train as far as Schaffhausen, where the German guarded train of an eight-compartment carriage and a baggage car awaited them. They travelled by way of Singen (where the train was stabled for the first night), Stuttgart, Frankfurt and Berlin to Sassnitz on the German island of Rügen, the port for ferries to Trelleborg in Sweden. A train took them to Stockholm, another the 600 miles (965 km) to the Swedish/Finnish border and a final train to St Petersburg, where Lenin arrived at the Finland station on 16 April. In July he had to flee Russia for Finland to avoid arrest. For a second time he crossed back into Russia by train on 9 August, and the locomotive that hauled both trains, No. 293, was presented by Finland to the Soviet Union and is preserved at the station.

HARVEST TRAINS ACROSS THE PRAIRIES

Many of Canada's small prairie towns are proud of their history and have a small museum spanning the century or so since their establishment. The museum at Outlook in Saskatchewan is in the former Canadian Pacific station building and contains a written account of these trains. Before mechanisation of wheat harvesting, huge numbers of workers were required to bring in the crop across the prairies. Special trains were operated to take workers from Ontario and the maritime provinces west in search of employment for the harvest.

The trains were vital for the farmers but dreaded by the townspeople, for they developed a reputation for bringing trouble. The railway soon learned to provide their worst carriages, since little respect was shown for windows or fittings. Trains would arrive in Winnipeg without a pane of glass intact. At each station, local farmers would meet the train and negotiate pay and conditions on the platform; those who accepted an offer got off, while those who thought they'd get a better offer continued west. It was not unknown for the destruction wreaked on the trains to be continued in towns, especially by those left without a position.

MEETING THE NEWSPAPER TRAIN

Newspapers and mail often went together in the same train, so Royal Mail staff and newsagents would often meet on the platform to await arrival of a train in the small hours. A Kendal newsagent recalled how as a boy he had to help his father from May 1908, meeting the train at 4.55am before going to school at 9am.

COMPANY WORKS OUTINGS

During the 19th century it became increasingly common for the larger and more enlightened employers to arrange excursions for their workforce. One of the first to do so was the woollen manufacturer Sir Titus Salt, founder of the Yorkshire model community of Saltaire, who in 1848 (when barricades were going up all over Europe) took 2,000 of his employees for a day's rambling among the woods and fields of Craven.

Blackpool was the destination for many of the mill-town excursions during Wakes Week, when maintenance was carried out on the mill machinery. For some reason the equivalent for engineering companies, including railway workshops, became known as Trip Weeks. At Swindon it entailed the use of 500 carriages to move 21,000 men, women and children to various West Country resorts. Families from the Caledonian Railway's works at St Rollox were taken for a day across the border in Carlisle, where the mayor had asked the populace to decorate houses and shops and put up signs saying 'Welcome to the St Rollox Visitors'.

Other firms organising such days were Reading biscuit maker Huntley & Palmer and Lever Brothers at Port Sunlight in Cheshire, but probably the best known works excursions were the Bass & Co. trains from Burton-on-Trent to such destinations as Blackpool and Great Yarmouth. In 1893, 15 trains were required, the first leaving at 3.50am for a pre-breakfast arrival in Great Yarmouth, where Bass employees

RAILWAY SIGNS

A working instruction notice of the Highland Railway, *c.*1920: 'ALL TRAIN CREWS WORKING THE PERTH ASYLUM BRANCH MUST ENSURE THAT ANY SIGNALS GIVEN TO THEM ARE BY RAILWAY STAFF.'

were cautioned by the company to 'avoid messes and odds and ends, the rather partaking of MEALS at proper hours as you do when at your ordinary employment'. Employees were provided with a guidebook to accompany each excursion, written by the Bass employee who organised them.

TRAIN CHARTERS

Organisations chartering a whole train could place considerable strain on resources, but railway companies seemed to rise to the challenge. In 1910, 250 teachers from Christ Church Sunday Schools in Sowerby Bridge wished to go to Hereford for the day; the London & North Western Railway provided a train of 11 dining-cars on which breakfast was served to all at 6.30am (after a 4am departure), and on the return journey dinner was served at 7.15pm, 15 minutes after departure from Hereford.

Even on service trains where one or two carriages were reserved for a party, extra facilities could be laid on. For 80 members of the Incorporated Municipal Electricians' Association travelling from London to Scotland, the LNWR laid on a whist drive and a concert.

FOWL DEMONSTRATION

One of the most curious exhibition trains run in Britain was the Great Eastern Railway's Egg and Poultry Demonstration Train of six adapted carriage vans and a restaurant car, which toured East Anglia in 1916. Its purpose was 'to improve trade conditions after the war' by encouraging the farmer, small-holder and cottager to take up the related industries. Lectures were delivered in conjunction with the exhibition. Its first tour of 22 stations was so successful, with 45,796 visitors, that a second tour was arranged.

PROHIBITION SPECIALS

A year after Prohibition began in the US in 1920, councillors in the town of Wick thought it time that temperance came to Caithness and closed the town's licensed premises. Many of Wick's citizens copied the US and took to bootlegging, but the Highland Railway was happy to provide a service for those who preferred a legitimate drink. Saturday specials were laid on for Lybster, the station once furthest from London by rail.

KEEP IT OUT OF THE SUN

An improvement in urban diet was one of the major benefits of railway transport through the availability of fresh produce. Paradoxically, milk wasn't one of the immediate improvements. Because trading was often done on station platforms and the milk was transferred from wholesalers' cans to retailers' cans, there was a greater risk of contamination and adulteration than with milk bought from an urban dairy where cows were kept. Milk was carried from 1832 on the Liverpool & Manchester Railway, but cows continued to be kept in cities until the network was fully developed and passenger trains could deliver milk quickly from up to 25 miles away. Standards of hygiene improved, and an outbreak of cattle plague in 1865–7 hastened the process of longer-distance sourcing. New urban markets for milk had an impact on rural prices. The higher prices paid by city retailers diverted supply and meant scarcity and higher prices locally.

Cooling of the milk before transit was begun in purposely built rail-served depots, the first opening at Semley in Dorset in 1871, and helped by specially ventilated vans. The first dedicated milk trains began running in the 1890s, and by the First World War 96 per cent of the capital's milk was delivered by rail, with a similar figure for provincial cities. Milk cans (or churns) were replaced by glass-lined or stainless-steel tank wagons, delivering bulk supplies to urban bottling plants such as the London depots at Cricklewood, South Acton, Vauxhall and Wood Lane.

The sound of milk churns being manhandled was probably the noisiest operation passengers witnessed at stations. Wartime rationalisation of distribution patterns was imposed by the Milk Marketing Board from 1942, and the last milk train ran in 1980.

CHRISTMAS DAY TRAINS

A train service was provided on Christmas Day until the 1950s. For Christmas 1931, the London & North Eastern Railway publicised the traditional Christmas Day lunch that would be served on the 'Flying Scotsman'. Stockings for children were provided on sleeping-car trains, though how the absence of a chimney for Santa Claus was explained has not been recorded.

JELLICOE COAL SPECIALS

During the First World War the Grand Fleet at Scapa Flow in the Orkney Islands required prodigious quantities of dry steam coal, which was produced only in the collieries of the Rhondda Valley and its immediate surroundings. It produced a high calorific value, but most importantly it was relatively smoke-free. Owing to the risk to coastal shipping from U-boats, trains were used to take part of the coal supplies to the northern ports of Glasgow, Newcastle, Grangemouth, Immingham and Hull. Between 27 August 1914 and 31 December 1918, a total of 13,631 special trains of Admiralty coal were operated. At an average train length of 40 wagons, with 10 tons per wagon, that amounts to about 5,452,400 tons of coal. The Shrewsbury & Hereford line was the major conduit from the valleys, but some were also routed over the single-line Brecon & Merthyr, Mid-Wales and Central Wales lines with their severe gradients and sharp curves.

A NIGHT ON THE TOWN

A story from the former Glasgow & South Western Railway driver David Smith illustrates the happy-go-lucky nature of early railway workings. The southern terminus of the Stranraer line in south-west Scotland was then Girvan, so the story must relate to the years before 1870. It was customary on the Saturday night of Glasgow Fair for an excursion to take the folk of Ayr south to Girvan 'for a change of drink'. It was past midnight when the train left Girvan, and it is unlikely the engine crew had been drinking tea all evening. Climbing Crosshill bank north of Kilkerran, they ran out of steam and stopped for a blow-up, putting on the blower to draw the fire. They sat down to wait for the pressure to rise and promptly fell asleep. Everyone in the train was evidently also in the land of nod, for it was dawn when the crew woke – to find the fire out. Kindling was cut in a nearby wood and the fire resuscitated. Steam was raised and they crept back into Ayr just as the first people were stirring. No word was heard about it.

CHAPTER EIGHT

RAILWAY OPERATIONS

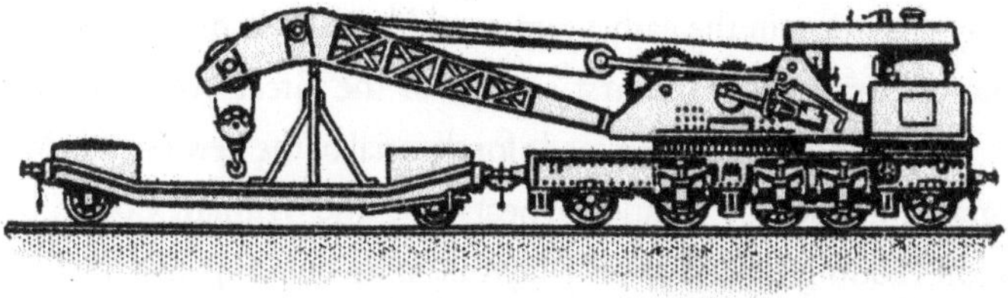

THERE HAVE BEEN few, if any, organisations as diverse and complex as railway companies at their most expansive. Quite apart from the many disciplines and functions required to operate a safe railway system, railway companies became involved with such areas as trams, buses, air transport, shipping, docks, warehousing, hotels, restaurants, steelmaking and publishing. Railway operating practice has been refined over almost two centuries, always in tandem with technological developments that have the potential to make train operation safer. It requires an exceptional degree of co-operation between staff and understanding of other people's jobs to run a railway efficiently. The railway is no place for compartmentalised thinking. However, most 21st-century railways are much more straightforward than they were even 50 years ago, when they carried much more diverse traffic calling for specialist rolling stock and complicated procedures. For example, many station and goods yard staff would have to know the handling requirements of a host of different animals, from pigeons to bulls.

CONTROL BY TELEGRAPH

It was fortuitous that construction of the first railways coincided with the first developments of the telegraph. Without it, or something comparable, railway operation in the early years would have been much less safe. Even before the opening of the first section of the Great Western Railway in 1838, arrangements had been made for the trial of the new Electric Magnetic Telegraph, devised by Charles Wheatstone and William Cooke, between London Paddington and West Drayton. At its own expense the GWR laid the five wires, insulated with cotton and gutta-percha, in an iron pipe above the ground beside the line. The agreement envisaged that the railway would be entitled to install the invention, if it proved successful, throughout the railway. The five-needle telegraph instruments at Paddington attracted immediate attention, being visited by the Duke of Wellington, Lord Bathurst and Lord Howick in August 1839. In 1842–3 the system was overhauled using two-needle instruments and wires suspended from cast-iron poles 10–25 ft (3–7.6 m) high, and extended to Slough.

What really captured the public imagination was the use made of the telegraph on New Year's Day in 1845. That day John Tawell of Berkhamsted had travelled from Paddington to Slough, intent on murdering his mistress, Sarah Hart, using prussic acid in a glass of stout. Having administered the lethal dose, he hastily returned to the station, but the victim's dying screams were heard by neighbours. Tawell was seen and a description of him, 'a man in the garb of a Kwaker' (there was no Q in the code at that time) was telegraphed to Paddington. From there he was followed and arrested at a coffee house. Tawell was convicted and publicly hanged at Aylesbury.

THE RAILWAY HORSE

During much of the 19th century probably as many horses were owned by the railway companies as by farmers. They were used to haul trains, shunt wagons and deliver goods by road. From 1901 motor vehicles began to replace the horse, but even in 1914 the 11 largest railway companies owned nearly 26,000 horses.

Stables were an intrinsic part of large goods yards. At London Paddington, there were so many horses that the stables were on two storeys with a covered ramp to the upper level. Many of the Great Western Railway's horses were purchased at the Lampeter Horse Fair, and the company held an annual competition for the 'finest horse' to encourage good care of them. Not all the stables were desirable residences, though: the horses that shunted the fish siding at Birmingham Snow Hill lived in a stable in the tunnel to the south of the station and rarely saw the light of day. Of course horses were labour-intensive: the 10 drays and 2 parcel horses at Kendal Station in Westmorland needed a foreman, 12 horsemen and 7 grooms.

Horses on a regular round soon needed no guidance or instruction. At Kendal the best of the parcel horses, Jane, knew her way around the town, would watch while a parcel was unloaded and delivered and then set off again.

ONE LUMP OR TWO?

Ponies were once used to haul platform trucks about the precincts of St Pancras station but the experiment was discontinued because, it was said, passengers became too friendly with the four-legged porters and distracted them from their duties with too many lumps of sugar.

Three Great Eastern Railway horses in Lowestoft were victims of the very first air raid of the First World War when an airship dropped three bombs.

NEVER ON THE SABBATH

Observance of the Lord's Day was one of the most controversial issues of the Victorian railway. The Liverpool & Manchester Railway established a precedent when it decided no train should leave either terminus between 10am and 4pm. This was widely adopted and became known as the 'church interval'. In 1832 one of the railway's directors was horrified to see a locomotive being repaired on a Sunday; an order was made that only in urgent cases should work be carried out on the sabbath. The LMR even went so far as to set up a separate fund for the net profits from trains worked on Sunday; this would be used for charitable purposes, as it was felt that the railway should not profit from Sunday operations.

Nowhere was opposition to Sunday trains greater than in the Highlands of Scotland, and matters came to a head in June 1883 when 'Wee Frees' (members of the fundamentalist minority within the Free Church) decided to enforce their strict Sabbatarian code. The herring season was in full swing, and boats from east coast ports had joined the Stornoway fleet to make the most of the short season; their crews had no scruples about working on Sunday. Three east coast boats eased up Loch Carron in the small hours of Sunday 3 June, and their crews were puzzled by fires glowing in the hills and along the shore.

The three boats landed at Strome Ferry pier and the work began of transferring the fish boxes on to the waiting train. Out of the dark a force of 50 men swooped on to the porters and disabled the crane with fists flying. By dawn 150 protestors guarded the pier, and the arguments of the stationmaster were of no avail. The solitary policeman at Plockton was powerless against such a force, and an assault by railwaymen and half a dozen constables sent by special train from Dingwall was soon repulsed. The Sabbatarians sang a psalm of victory.

At midnight their force melted away, and loading of the train resumed. The threat of a repeat performance the following Sunday was taken sufficiently seriously that the matter was on the desk of the Home Secretary. Constables from all over Scotland were dispatched to Strome Ferry, and a troop train with 70 soldiers and four officers from Edinburgh Castle was sent to Fort George to stand ready to move west should the need arise. The knowledge of it, coupled with the large police force, was enough to deter even the 400-odd protestors who assembled near Strome Ferry on the Saturday. Police protection continued throughout June, and there was no further obstruction of railway traffic.

In 1899 the Great North of Scotland Railway was criticised for encouraging people 'to desecrate the Sabbath day by playing golf' at its new hotel on Cruden Bay, but opinion was softening. The local paper defended the railway, for 'beguiling a lot of idle fellows out to Cruden Bay, where I am sure they will be just as well employed in playing golf on Sundays as loafing about church doors and annoying worshippers, as they are complained of doing in Aberdeen.'

In fact for much of the century it suited the railway companies not to operate passenger trains on Sunday, as they were generally run at a loss in the days before widespread weekend travel. As leisure time increased, objection to Sunday trains diminished, but as late as 1909 the Rev Lord Blythswood of the Lord's Day Observance Society said that he would never set foot on a train on the sabbath.

FREIGHT IS GREAT (*STARLIGHT EXPRESS*)

It is hard today to credit how much freight the railways once moved, before road transport was allowed its hegemony. In 1905 alone 236 million tons of coal was mined, and most of it was moved by rail in 10-ton coal wagons. To take one example, in March 1928 the Tredegar Iron & Coal Co. received or dispatched 8,559 wagons. Coal output had been in decline for years by the outbreak of the Second World War, but there were still 589,000 privately owned coal wagons belonging to 3,947 different owners – before nationalisation of the coal industry most coal was moved in wagons owned by the collieries or coal merchants. As late as 1956, each week would see about 330,000 loaded wagons leave 800 pits and open-cast coal sites.

So much sugar beet was produced in East Anglia during the 1946–7 season that the regional factories could not cope, and 1,179,063 of the 4½ million tons was moved in 126,882 wagon loads to beet sugar factories in Lincolnshire and the East Midlands.

During the years when politicians thought oil would last for ever and hacked back the rail network with an unforgivable lack of prescience, countless transport arrangements dating back a century were disrupted. Strawberry growers in the Cheddar and Tamar valleys, for example, lamented the loss of the branch lines that took away their produce, because they found that road transport bruised the fruit much more than rail.

THE OCEAN'S BOUNTY

Fish was one of the most perishable commodities transported by rail, and some companies such as the Highland Railway allowed fully braked fish wagons to be included in passenger trains. Grimsby was one of the largest trawler ports, and even in the late 1950s its Fish Dock would dispatch 330 wagons on a Monday and 250 on other weekdays.

During the winter of 1894–5 a severe blizzard hit the Highlands on 29 December, and at some time or other during the next two months every part of its main line from Perth to Wick/Thurso was snowbound, except the Inverness–Helmsdale section. One of the first trains to become stuck fast was a herring special from Wick, which came to grief at a notorious spot named Fairy Hillocks near Altnabreac. It was 10 days before the train was dug out, but its contents were still in perfect condition.

WHAT'S IN A NAME?

Signal-boxes on the Great Western Railway carried a cast-iron plate beneath the lineside windows bearing their name, followed by the words 'Signal Box'. The box at the Wiltshire station of Box therefore had a plate reading 'Box Signal Box'.

BELLS RING FOR BEER

Brewery railways once threaded the flat urban landscape of Burton-on-Trent to such an extent that around 1900 there were 32 level crossings and a similar number of signal-boxes in the town. Bells warned pedestrians that the gates were about to be closed to allow a saddletank – in 'Turkey red' from Bass or olive green from Ind Coope & Allsopp – to puff importantly across the street with a string of wagons. Hundreds of empty wagons would be stored for emergency use, in addition to the hundreds dispatched across the country in beer trains. Even as late as the mid 1960s there were 16 departures between 4pm and 2.53am.

SUBTERFUGE IN THE WELSH MARCHES

One of the railways for which there was never what we would term a 'business case' was the Bishop's Castle Railway between the eponymous Shropshire market town and the main Shrewsbury & Hereford line at Craven Arms. Scenting a turkey, the local MP failed to turn up for the official opening in 1865, blaming the death of Lord Palmerston, and the railway spent most of its 70-year life in the hands of the receiver. Even the usual saviour of lost railway causes, Lieutenant-Colonel Holman Frederick Stephens (see page 230), declined to add the BCR to his portfolio of near-terminal cases. A sheriff in 1869 'could find no property to seize' to satisfy a court judgement against the railway for an outstanding debt.

One of the local landowners, Dr Frank Beddoes, had never pressed the railway for payment for the land he had released, regarding the railway as a public benefit and a few acres of land as neither here nor there. His executors took a different view. In 1877 bailiffs swooped on the railway and removed a section of rail near Horderley, and there they intended to remain until payment was made. After a week, supplies in Bishop's Castle were running low, and a local coal merchant called a secret council in a Craven Arms hostelry. All wagons at Craven Arms destined for Bishop's Castle were marshalled into a train, while a couple of men were charged with casually taking pity on the bailiffs and suggesting that the comfort of the Lion Inn would be preferable to a pointless evening beside the silent line.

A warm fire and a few gallons of beer laced with gin did the trick, and the bailiffs were oblivious to the sound of the locomotive creeping past over the hastily reinstated rails on its way from Bishop's Castle to Craven Arms. The bailiffs had recovered enough to hear the unavoidable bark of the engine on the return journey with wagons of supplies, but their waving lanterns and shouts were not going to stop the train. Lawyers threatened the railway's manager, but he had an alibi, and they evidently decided that the game was not worth the candle and let the railway's receiver carry on with his rather half-hearted efforts to balance the books.

FOUR-LEGGED FRIENDS

Many stations had a cat or dog informally attached to the staff. Until its closure to passengers in 1959, the Devon terminus at Moretonhampstead had a memorial to a cat that seems to have been chosen for its rodent-catching abilities: 'Beneath this slab, and stretched out flat, lies Jumbo, once our station cat.'

THE LAST RAILWAY HORSE

At nationalisation in 1948, British Railways still employed about 9,000 horses, mostly delivering goods from stations. A few were employed in moving rail wagons at goods yards, and Britain's last railway horse, a 24-year-old bay with white feather named Charlie, was retired on 21 February 1967 from shunting duties at Newmarket goods yard. Appropriately, he had spent his six years at Newmarket moving horse-boxes containing his racing cousins. Charlie was in the parade of horse personalities at the Horse of the Year show at Wembley in 1965, and was retired to the fields of Clare Hall near Bath, then home of an also retired railway officer.

BATTLING SNOW

The solutions to the problem of snow have been broadly similar: snow-ploughs of various kinds and snow sheds across the line to protect it from avalanches. At places susceptible to snowdrifts the Highland Railway of Scotland tried with some success 'snow blowers' – angled wood panels beside the line that channelled the wind to blow snow off the track. But in most cases there was no substitute for brute force: three or four locomotives would be coupled together with a large snowplough at each end and they would charge the drift. Railwaymen who remember such events say there was no more thrilling sight and sound on the railway. One of the most popular films made by British Transport Films, *Snowdrift at Bleath Gill* (1955), captures the drama of the moment as well as the hard slog of digging out a snowbound train between Kirkby Stephen and Barnard Castle. This line had been severely affected by the weather in the spring of 1947, when the railway was frozen up for over eight weeks, and J21 0–6–0 No. 5090 was stranded in a cutting near Belah Viaduct throughout that time.

The most effective solution has been the rotary snowplough or blower. The concept and the main elements of today's ploughs were dreamed up by a Toronto dentist, J.W. Elliott, who took out a patent in 1869 for a 'compound revolving snow shovel'. With various refinements, the first full-size plough was built by the Cooke Locomotive

Works in New Jersey and put to work in Iowa on the lines of the Chicago & North Western Railway in 1885–6. By the early 20th century, steam-powered rotary snow-blowers were being widely used in countries such as Canada and Switzerland.

ANIMALS ON THE MOVE

In the days when Britain's railways were legally obliged to carry any consignment, all manner of animals had to be carried, sometimes posing a challenge to station and train staff. Passenger trains would carry dogs, cats, goats, cockerels, pigeons, ferrets, rabbits, crabs, lobsters and even maggots for anglers. Staff were instructed to be careful where they tied the label; too often the animal chewed it up. More than one porter has chased a dog making a bid for freedom, shouting, 'Stop that dog, it's a parcel!' The number of rabbits dispatched from Bridestowe (pronounced 'Briddystoe') on Dartmoor was said to exceed the number of passengers. Boxes of them were sent away in the days when warrening was still one of the occupations for the moor's inhabitants.

Stock sales generated huge volumes of traffic and placed a major burden on often limited facilities. Autumn sheep sales at Lairg and Thurso in the Highlands might see as many as 30,000 sheep sold in a day, requiring up to 10 special trains to the south.

MAKING A BEE LINE

A traveller on the Ravenglass & Eskdale Railway in August 1906, before it was converted from 3 ft to 15 in gauge, remembered the train containing a carriage full of beehives. Stops were made between stations for the guard to position one, two or three hives wherever he judged the bees would make good heather honey.

BROAD-GAUGE GOODS VANS

A Great Western Railway employee, who worked as a goods guard for the last 22 years of broad-gauge operation, recalled talking to a guard in the 1860s about the very early days, when brake vans were entirely open and simply had a brake handle projecting up through the floor of the wagon. Even when later broad-gauge brake vans received a roof, they were made entirely of iron, lacked the comfort of a stove, and guards would scrounge straw from goods sheds to provide some insulation.

BATTLING THE GRADE

The battle between gravity and the skill and stamina of the footplate crew was played out daily at countless places around the world. Steep inclines that produce the greatest aural and visual display of power from steam locomotives have always attracted spectators. In Britain places such as the Dainton, Shap and Beattock inclines have been irresistible to photographers since the time when cameras could capture trains at speed, but only the Lickey Incline in Worcestershire could rival some overseas grades in requiring up to five locomotives to heave a single train over the summit. Comparable numbers were required on the climb to Soldier Summit in Utah on the Denver & Rio Grande Western Railroad, which could require no fewer than four locomotives at the front and a banker (or 'helper' as they were termed in the US) at the rear. Perhaps the toughest challenge of all was on the line through the Bolan Pass to Quetta on the North Western Railway in what is now Pakistan; the footplate crews often worked in searing temperatures as up to four locomotives struggled up mile after mile of 1 in 25 with heavy mail trains.

DENVER & RIO GRANDE WESTERN
SCENIC LINE OF THE WORLD

THE LAST SLIP COACH

To serve stations without the loss of time taken to slow, stop and regain running speed, British railway companies used the slip coach. A slip coupling allowed the rear carriage of the train to detach itself from the train at a precise point in advance of a station, and a guard controlled the freewheeling approach to stop the coach at the platform while the rest of the train continued its journey without loss of speed.

The first deployment of slip coaches is thought to have been on the London & Greenwich Railway in 1840, using detachable rope couplings. More sophisticated apparatus was used in February 1858 at Hayward's Heath on the London Brighton & South Coast Railway, when a portion for Eastbourne was slipped. The most enthusiastic user of slip coaches was the Great Western Railway, which slipped its first coaches at Slough and Banbury on the way from London Paddington to Birmingham in December 1858. GWR slip services reached a peak in 1908, when there were 79. By 1914 this had fallen to 60, though 10 other railway companies had adopted the facility, making a total of 176 slip-coach services in the August 1914 edition of Bradshaw's guide. Although slip coaches enabled a train to serve more destinations in a shorter time, they required a guard for each slip coach, could not pick up passengers in the same way and their occupants could not use a dining-car. The last slip coach drew to a halt at Bicester on 9 September 1960.

The idea was adopted for a small number of services by a few other countries such as France, Holland and Ireland.

GRAND TRUNK RAILWAY,

BUFFALO AND GODERICH DIVISION.

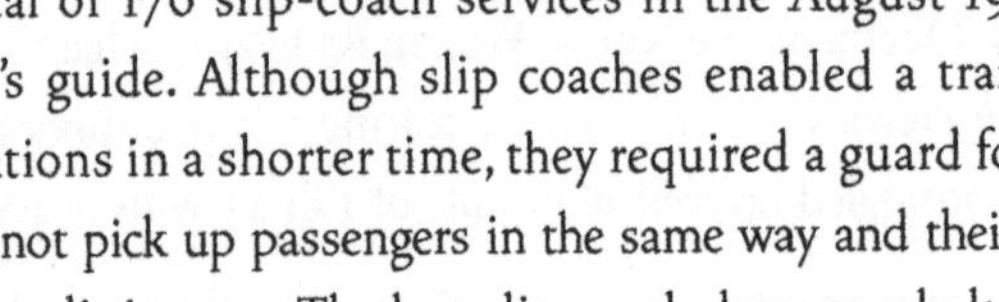

SUPERINTENDENT'S OFFICE,

BRANTFORD, C. W.

OFF THE RAILS

It was a ruse of engine shed cleaners on a quiet night duty to take a nap in the firebox of a locomotive, which probably provided residual warmth if not comfort. On at least one occasion, this had near-fatal results when a shovelful of live coals was thrown into the firebox to start the fire.

FRENCH RAILWAY RESISTANCE

The 1946 documentary film *La Bataille du Rail* and the 1964 thriller *The Train*, starring Burt Lancaster and Paul Scofield, are vivid portrayals of the work of French railwaymen in obstructing the smooth operation of the SNCF under Nazi occupation during the Second World War. Passive resistance was the most widespread form – documents were lost, urgently needed wagons inexplicably diverted to wrong destinations, administration obfuscated – but as D-Day approached, sabotage became more common. In the Lyons district alone there were 568 incidents in the first eight months of 1944, of which 260 resulted in the complete immobilisation of traffic.

ARTERIES OF THE NATION

It is axiomatic that until motor vehicles began to erode their traffic, railways were the conduit of most movements of people and freight. A comparison of just one cross-country railway illustrates the point. Today the scenic Central Wales line sees four passenger trains every weekday in each direction between Shrewsbury and Swansea and no freight. In 1911 the line had 160 train movements, of which 18 were up passenger trains and 19 down, with the rest devoted to freight. This included northbound trains conveying 6,000 tons a week, and there was an overnight beer train from Burton-on-Trent. Even as late as 1960, the line still had 32 private siding connections, albeit some with little or no traffic. Before the First World War, the line had through trains or carriages to and from London, Manchester, Liverpool, Leeds, Huddersfield and York, helped by the popularity of the line's four spas. Llandrindod Wells, in what was then Radnorshire, was the busiest, with 100,000 visitors a year, and it sometimes took 15 minutes for hotel porters to unload the voluminous quantities of luggage with which tourists of the day travelled.

CONGESTED ARTERIES

Managing capacity to cope with the traffic on offer has been a perennial challenge on the railway. Some leeway has to be built into the timetable so that the delay of one train does not have a domino effect on all others. For most of their history, there has not been enough capacity on Britain's railways; during the brief period when politicians (and some railwaymen) thought the day of the railway was past, capacity was reduced by such measures as singling double lines and scaling back signalling. This is having to be reversed.

The first two decades of the 20th century saw Britain's railways under immense strain, none more so than the Midland Railway where coal trains made pitiful progress south from the Yorkshire coalfields towards the capital. Sometimes an engine crew would book on and not turn a wheel because of congestion. Signalmen were reprimanded if they delayed a passenger train, so they took no risks with slow-moving coal trains, which crept south from goods loop to goods loop. The lack of telephone communication made it difficult for headquarters at Derby to know where a train had got to, never mind arrange for the relief of its crew when they might be in a remote loop in the countryside. In 1907 there were 20,000 cases of train crew working excessive hours.

This congestion not only affected the running of the railway, but the delay in returning empty wagons to collieries was damaging their operations. The man who sorted this out was Cecil Paget, General Superintendent of the MR, who studied train movements from a carriage in which he camped beside the railway at Rotherham Masborough. He set up a permanent control office at this important junction, implemented new procedures and extended the responsibilities of district control offices. Key signal-boxes reported train movements on a regular basis, both to help planning and so that crew relief could be organised. This had a major impact on a demoralised workforce, and in 1911 there was not a single case of excessive hours being worked.

But the greatest legacy of Paget's reforms was the idea of trains having 'paths' in the timetable, and the method of devising timetables using lines on squared graph paper became the norm until the computer.

GUESTS TO CRUDEN BAY

One of the most unusual railways in Scotland was the electric tramway on the Aberdeenshire coast linking the station at Cruden Bay with the Cruden Bay Hotel. Built by the Great North of Scotland Railway and opened in 1899 with its own specially designed golf course, the hotel catered primarily for golfers. The red granite 96-bedroomed hotel was ¾ mile (1.2 km) from the station, so a 3 ft 6½ in gauge electric tramway was built to take guests to the door of the 'palace in the sandhills' as it was dubbed. The two cars were built at the GNSR's works at Kittybrewster, Aberdeen, and seated 16, with space for laundry baskets and luggage. In the kitchens French and Italian chefs were employed, and the waitresses in navy-blue crêpe de Chine dresses were inspected before dinner every evening, particularly shoes and fingernails. Despite the early patronage of such magnates as Sir Jeremiah Colman (mustard), Sir William Burrell (ships), Thomas Wills (cigarettes), the McEwans (brewers) and Crawfords (biscuits), as well as politicians such as Harold Macmillan, Lloyd George and Asquith, the season was too short and the location too remote. After a twice-daily service by Rolls-Royce between the hotel and Aberdeen station was laid on in 1932, the tramway was used only for freight, mainly laundry and coal.

Even the branch line to Cruden Bay (and on to Boddam) closed to passengers in 1932, but the tramway survived to carry mostly laundry and coal until March 1941. The hotel served as a wartime hospital but was formally closed in November 1945. No buyer could be found and demolition was completed by 1952, while the golf course remains one of the best in Scotland.

THE DISRUPTION OF SNOW

The Highland Railway of Scotland was, not surprisingly, the British railway most affected by snow. Barely a winter of the 19th century passed without train running being affected, and some passengers had to endure considerable privation when their trains stuck fast in drifts. On 17 December 1880 a mixed train of passenger coaches and cattle and fish trucks became embedded in snow to the north of Dava station on the wild Morayshire moors between Forres and Aviemore. The crew and passengers made their way to Dava station, where they found other refugees from a train that had become stuck south of the station. After several days, provisions in the station house were exhausted by the unexpected guests, so permission was sought and granted by telegraph for the fish to be cooked.

A week later another blizzard struck Caithness, in the extreme north, and a train that departed from Wick on Saturday 24th became buried in 10 ft (3 m) of snow south of Scotscalder station. Four locomotives and a large snowplough with three teams of men were sent out to the rescue, but another blizzard snowed them in near Altnabreac. Not until Tuesday was contact made with the train, and the passengers were then taken to Thurso, but it was Thursday before the beleaguered train was finally released from the snow.

Even footplate crews accustomed to the elements resorted to extraordinary measures to minimise their discomfort. When a banking locomotive derailed while running downhill tender-first, it was discovered that the crew hadn't seen the snowdrift responsible because they weren't even on the footplate. They were trying to keep out of the wind by sheltering in front of the smokebox on the buffer beam. To control the locomotive's speed, they had devised the unorthodox method of opening the end of the brake pipe with a stout knife, thereby releasing the pressure and triggering the automatic brake.

In 1883 a southbound goods train with two locomotives became stuck south of Dava when their snowplough disintegrated. They improvised a shelter by removing tarpaulins from wagons of potatoes and rigged up a tent over the cab, keeping the fires going through the night. When dawn broke, they went to find the guard in his brake van and discovered him with two drovers and two other individuals who had been having an unauthorised ride south. They had broken the seal of a meat van and cooked themselves a meal of mutton and potatoes. The animals still alive were released from the vans. The men noticed a cottage in the distance and in making for it discovered a girl lying in the snow. They carried her to the cottage and found a woman and children who had been without food or heat for several days. The train became their refuge, but it was a full week before this motley company was rescued by teams from Inverness.

On Monday 28 December 1908, the 4.15pm Glasgow–Stranraer express of non-corridor coaches got into trouble in a cutting south of Barrhill and stuck fast. The snow was so deep that the fireman was able to hang the single-line tablet hoop on a telegraph pole cross-bar. There was no steam heating and the powdery snow seeped into the compartments. It was 11am the following day before a party from Barrhill struggled through the snow, and the only way food could be handed to the stranded passengers was through the holes in the roof for pot-lamps. A train of dock labourers from Ayr, drafted in to help, managed to leave open the doors of the carriages in which they travelled, so that too became a casualty of the still-falling snow. Seven engines were brought in to battle their way to the express, but it was

Wednesday before the doors on the lee-side were prised open and the passengers released and taken to Barrhill station.

DIVERSIFICATION INTO WICKER

Railways have often diversified into complementary activities, such as hotels, docks, warehousing, shipping, buses and even air services. Many produced their own stationery and all manner of supplies for railway premises and operations. An extreme instance of this was the London & North Western Railway's acquisition in 1880 of a basket-making company in Aylesbury. The LNWR built a new factory to the south of its station approaches. It grew osiers along the track of the branch to Cheddington on land purchased for a second line of rails which was never laid, as well as along other LNWR lines. The factory produced about 2,000 baskets a year from 1893, ranging from large hampers to baskets for correspondence and waste paper.

CHAPTER NINE

WORKING FOR THE RAILWAY

RAILWAYMEN HAVE A sense of camaraderie probably unrivalled by any other industry apart from the armed services. Railways rely on teamwork, order and discipline, so it is no surprise that many of its early officers were drawn from the army. The pre-eminence of 19th-century railways in society and in engineering made its servants part of the aristocracy of labour, reflected in the proud stance to be seen in photographs of railwaymen, whether on platforms or footplate. A position on the railways was greatly sought after, as much for job security (on most railways) as for the wages. A sense of loyalty worked both ways, preference often being given to applicants who had a member of the family working for the company. Working conditions were often hard, especially on the footplate for much of the 19th century when minimal protection from the elements was provided for the driver and fireman. Hours too were disgracefully long in occupations that required mental alertness for safety, until accidents forced their reduction.

OPPORTUNITIES FOR THE YOUNG

One of the less well covered aspects of railway history is the young age at which many were given responsible positions. Some senior appointments are well known: Daniel Gooch was made the first Locomotive Superintendent of the Great Western Railway at 20, while Brunel was just 26 when he was given the job of building it. But it also applied to much lower grades. A boy who joined the Great Central Railway in the 1880s at the age of 13 was made a foreman cleaner at 18, in charge of about 200 cleaners at Gorton, and by 21 was firing on express passenger trains.

CAREFUL AND INTELLIGENT WORKERS

The great French engineer Marc Seguin (1786–1875) complained of the difficulties he had in finding such men in France, whereas 'in England a worker needs to be told only once. He will then be able to carry out his task without further prompting.' This may have been partly because of the earlier industrialisation of Britain, but during the course of the 19th century the French greatly improved technical education, and the complexity of French locomotive design relied on the mechanical knowledge of French footplate crews to get the best out of them.

NO LOOPHOLES

The Beira Railway's 1898 book of Rules and Regulations wasn't leaving much room for argument when it stated: 'Every person employed by this Company must devote himself exclusively to its work; reside at whatever place may be appointed; attend at such hours as may be required; and pay prompt obedience to all persons in authority over him; and conform to all the rules and regulations of the Company.' The author of these diktats, Arthur Lawley, later opened the first brick-built hotel in Beira, the Savoy, where he presided with a similar rod of iron. Even Cecil Rhodes met his match in Lawley; years earlier when the statesman had started swearing at Lawley in his high-pitched voice in front of staff, Lawley asked him who the hell he thought he was and to stop squealing like a damned rabbit.

CRIME AND PUNISHMENT

Punitive fines on staff were a disagreeable aspect of Victorian railway life. Enginemen could be fined for all kinds of perceived shortcomings. Even on the Brill Tramway in Buckinghamshire, hardly the stamping ground of crack expresses, the rule book warned: 'If the train be late at Quainton Junction in consequence of a late Start, the fault of the driver not having his engine ready, a fine of Half a day's Pay to be imposed.'

LOOKING AFTER THE STAFF

On Sunday 22 September 1912, the pages of *Railway & Travel Monthly* reported a reception 'unique in the annals of the railway world other than those of the Stratford-on-Avon & Midland Junction Railway', held at Lord Willoughby de Broke's Warwickshire seat at Compton Verney. The directors of the railway invited the entire staff, and about 250 accepted.

The afternoon began with a service in the estate church, and the house and grounds were open to guests. A 'meat tea' was served to the strains of the Blakesley Silver Band.

BLOWING OFF ON SALARIES

A shareholder at an AGM of the London Midland & Scottish Railway in the 1930s was bold enough to challenge Lord Stamp on the size of the President's salary of £15,000. Stamp retorted that 'if you were to divide the £15,000 among all the shareholders, each of you wouldn't even get a ham sandwich.'

THE WEBB ORPHANAGE

As pre-welfare state employers, the railway companies were paternalistic in their approach, providing accommodation for a large proportion of their employees as well as various social and religious services where a concentration of employees justified them. With this went a strong sense of responsibility and philanthropy among some senior managers. Perhaps the most remarkable instance of this was the bequest in the will of Francis Webb (1836–1906), Chief Mechanical Engineer of the London & North Western Railway, who paid for the erection and endowment of a huge clock-towered orphanage in Crewe. With a frontage of 200 ft (61 m), the building provided accommodation for 40 orphans of LNWR employees, 20 of each sex, with a large playground and various day rooms and sitting-rooms.

SNOWDONIA STATIONMISTRESS

Probably the most frequently photographed railway official in Britain was Bessie Jones. In 1929 she married a Festiniog Railway porter at Tan-y-Bwlch, where they lived in the station house until their retirement in 1968. In the 1930s Bessie became stationmistress and made a point of meeting all trains dressed in Welsh national costume, until the railway closed in mid-September 1939. When the preserved Ffestiniog Railway reopened to Tan-y-Bwlch in 1958, Bessie resumed her work as stationmistress.

BRAVING THE WINTER

One of the worst winters on record was in 1947, when drifts on the trans-Pennine line between Barnard Castle and Kirkby Stephen reached a depth of 30 ft (9 m) at Barras in Westmorland. The signalmen at Stainmore summit and the porter in charge at Barras were unable to get home for over three weeks, and depended on food delivered by snowplough or military special from Barnard Castle. On 3 February a train from Kirkby Stephen became stuck fast in a drift and, together with two locomotives and two ploughs sent to rescue it, was embedded in snow for 17 days.

Elsewhere 200 German prisoners of war were employed trying to keep open Dunford Bridge marshalling yard between Penistone and Hadfield.

Another bad winter was 1963. Southern England rarely features in tales of snowed-in trains, but that year a tank engine sent out from Ilfracombe was so completely buried in a cutting that you could walk from bank to bank over the top of it.

CHRISTMAS CHEER

To brighten Christmas for children living in remote railway houses along the West Highland line in Scotland, a tradition began between the world wars of the District Engineer delivering toys by special train. In 1946 dolls' prams and mechanical toys (including a model railway) were delivered to 89 children in 36 houses between Craigendoran and Mallaig. Books were given to the parents.

THE ADVENT OF THE SKIRT

A rather bad poem of this title was written by a male clerk at the Railway Clearing House in 1912, when the first female clerks were taken on at the Seymour (later Eversholt) Street offices at Euston in London. The employment of the 24 young ladies was a radical step at the time, though only two years later the First World War would transform the ratio of sexes on the railway, at least for the duration of the conflict. A trade magazine reported that 'great interest is manifested by the ordinary staff... in the innovation'.

In fact, it was not the first example of the employment of women on the railway. Following the nationalisation of the telegraph in 1869, the Post Office attracted many male telegraphists from the railways, and the North British Railway responded by training women to 'manipulate the instruments'. Other railways followed suit, and Anthony Trollope wrote a short story reflecting the trend, 'The Telegraph Girl'.

There cannot have been a railway that did not rely on female staff during the First World War. Miss Annie Johnston became the first female employee of the Maryport & Carlisle Railway when she became a clerk at Aspatria station in 1915 on six shillings (30p) a week. She was told that it would be only for the duration of the war, but within two years she was a travelling ticket inspector on 22s 6d (£1 12½p) and she did not retire from railway service until 1958. In 1917 the Lancashire & Yorkshire Railway went so far as to appoint a station *mistress* at Irlams-o'-th'-Height station, where all the other staff were women.

From 1917, the Great Western Railway 'even' had a female constable: Miss Annie Eva Martin is thought to have been the first female special constable on any railway and swore before the Stipendiary Magistrate at Marylebone Police Court to 'well and truly serve our Sovereign Lord the King in the office of special constable within the premises of the Great Western Railway Company, and, to the best of my power, cause the peace to be kept and preserved, and to prevent all offences against the person and properties of His Majesty's subjects.'

All was not plain sailing. The North Eastern Railway trained some women to become signalwomen, but the signalmen and drivers threatened to strike if they were employed. The male staff of the NER were no keener on the idea of clergy getting involved with the railway, even in wartime. Four clergymen qualified as signalmen during the First World War, but protests were made through the union, and again the move was blocked.

GRAND
TRUNK
RAILWAY
SYSTEM

UNSOCIABLE HOURS

The long hours that early railwaymen were expected to work became an immediate cause of contention, vis-à-vis the wages they were paid. In the first year of operation, the Liverpool & Manchester Railway expected its policemen – in effect signalmen standing beside the line with flags and lamps and nothing more than a wooden sentry box for shelter – to work 16 hours a day. They were paid 17s 6d (87½p) a week. Goods clerks fared no better, receiving £60 a year for a day that began at 6am and ended at 10pm. In 1831 they managed to negotiate an increase to £80 per annum. Demarcation disputes plagued industrial life even then: the policemen considered it no part of their duty to assist an engine crew by operating hand-thrown points (before centralised control of points and signals from a signal-box), but they were told they must.

Long hours continued to be a problem on the railways, especially in 'safety critical' occupations. F.S. Williams in his 1876 history of the Midland Railway refers to a goods train driver who in 1870–71 had on at least 36 occasions worked 15 hours or more; and on one occasion he was in charge of a locomotive for 28 hours without a break. It wasn't much better for station staff. A level-crossing keeper at Cononley, just south of Skipton in Yorkshire, was on duty from 6.30am until the last train left at 9.59pm, and besides the gates he was expected

OFF THE RAILS

The risk of sudden floods on the railway through the Usage swamps on the main line between Dar-es-Salaam and Lake Tanganyika was so great that in the mid 1960s locomotive crews were issued with inflatable life-jackets.

to help unload goods and, since there was no porter, attend the 19 passenger trains that called there. During the night the gates were closed to road traffic, but he had to get up to open them on demand, usually twice a night but often as many as seven times.

David L. Smith in his reminiscences of the Glasgow & South Western Railway tells of Stranraer enginemen arriving home after a return trip to Carlisle, only to find a train of fish waiting. 'Nae engine for the fish. Get some coal and away back to Carlisle!' Turns of 36 hours were not unknown. A series of articles published in the *Daily Telegraph* in 1871 as a result of intensive research brought home forcibly the long hours culture on the railway, revealing that guards were commonly on duty for 90 hours a week and that it was 'by no means rare' to do 100. A guard at Leeds had worked 18 hours when he was told to take a train to London. The exhausted man asked the superintendent how many hours he was expected to work and received the reply: 'That's our business. You've got 24 hours in a day like every other man, and they are all ours if we want you to work them.'

Reform came slowly, accelerated by accidents such as the disaster at Thirsk in 1892, caused by a signalman's exhaustion. He had been up all night with a sick daughter who died, and after he fell asleep a southbound express ploughed into the back of a stationary goods train. In May 1894 the Highland Railway issued a notice advising: 'In future Enginemen and Firemen who have worked 12 hours at a stretch will, if they so wish, telegraph to the Foreman to be relieved at the first Locomotive Depot at which they are due to arrive.'

RAILWAY SIGNS

Railway companies sometimes employed euphemistic language to influence behaviour. When in 1910 the Great Western Railway introduced steam rail motor services between Hallatrow and Limpley Stoke on the Somerset/Wiltshire border, it put up a handbill which read: 'THE COMPANY HAVE THE GREATEST DESIRE TO MAKE THE MOTOR CAR SERVICE PUNCTUAL, AND THE PUBLIC CAN VERY MATERIALLY ASSIST IN THAT DIRECTION IF THEY WILL BE ALERT IN GETTING IN AND OUT OF THE CARS.' This section of railway later gained fame as the setting for the film *The Titfield Thunderbolt.*

ZEBRAS, ACTORS AND TORTOISES

The instructions given to Britain's railway staff became ever more detailed as the 19th century progressed, as it tried to provide an answer for every eventuality. To take the 1903 Great Central Railway timetable, it helpfully stipulated that 'Camels and Zebras conveyed in Horse Boxes are charged at the Horse rate, according to the number of stalls occupied.' The 'Owners' Risk Scale of Rates for the Conveyance of Perishable and Certain Other Traffics by Passenger Train' lists such disparate items as haggis, sausage skins, seeds for birds, and sheep fleeces. Items for carriage in the Guard's Van included Polish for Ballroom Floors and Engines of Steam Roundabouts, and it was thought necessary to advise that 'Tramway Cars will not be carried by Passenger Trains'. Perhaps in acknowledgement of the amount of theatre companies travelling the country, the theatrical profession was generously treated at Great Central Railway cloakrooms; their private luggage was charged half the ordinary rate.

This complexity was satirised by *Punch* in about 1890. The cartoon showed a country station porter scratching his head and, with a tortoise in the other hand, addressing an elderly lady whose pets he is trying to classify: 'Stationmaster, he says, dogs is dogs, and cats is dogs, and rabbits is dogs, but this 'ere tortoise, he's an insect, so I reckon there be'ant no charge for 'im, ma'am.'

THE FOG SIGNALMAN

The work of the fog signalman is a task that has entirely disappeared from the railway, and not one that is missed. Usually drawn from permanent way staff but supplemented by goods shed porters and locomotive depot cleaners, fog signalmen were assigned to specific signals to show drivers whether or not the signal was at danger. In thick fog the position of the signal arm or the colour of the illuminated signal glass would of course be shrouded in fog, especially on main lines, where posts were often made taller to improve sighting in normal weather. The fog signalman would have a small hut like a sentry box and a coal brazier beside it, and he would place detonators on the line when the signal was at danger and remove them when all clear. The detonators exploded under the wheels of locomotives, alerting the driver to stop. It was a disagreeable occupation, working on one's own in the cold with minimal visibility, but vital to the safe running of the railway at its most vulnerable.

KEEPING UP APPEARANCES

Railway staff dealing with passengers were and are the public face of the industry, so presentation matters. Staff who allowed their appearance to fall below the standard expected were liable to be reprimanded. On 18 December 1919, the stationmaster at Achterneed in Ross & Cromarty received a letter from the Traffic Manager's Office in Inverness: 'It is reported that your pointsman was wearing a tweed cap when examining tickets on 11 a.m. [train] of 15th inst. Please say as to this.'

FOUR-LEGGED FRIENDS

A part of South Australian railway folklore is Bob, a long-haired dog of rather indeterminate pedigree who quit his role of rabbit catcher at Quorn for the railway. He was adopted by a porter at Petersburg named William Ferry, who taught him tricks, and when Ferry was made a guard Bob went with him on the train. This lifestyle so suited Bob that when Ferry was promoted to Assistant Station Master at Petersburg, Bob preferred to carry on travelling, choosing to sit on the tender in front of the coal. On his collar was a brass plate inscribed with the request: 'Stop me not, but let me jog / For I am Bob, the driver's dog'. After Bob's death in 1895, the collar was saved by the Australian Federated Union of Locomotive Enginemen and is now on display in the National Railway Museum in Port Adelaide.

COMPANY RIVALRY

There was intense rivalry between the railway companies that were grouped together in 1923 into the 'Big Four', and in the quarter-century before nationalisation in 1948 a sense of the superiority of one's own company could frustrate progress when old company loyalties clouded rational decision-making. Among Scottish companies, there was little love lost between the Glasgow & South Western and Caledonian railways. The persistence of this feeling is illustrated by an anecdote from November 1936, when news came through of the abdication of Edward VIII. The whole country was in a state of uncertainty about this unprecedented event, and knots of railwaymen were discussing the matter that evening at Ayr station on the former GSWR. An inspector leaned confidentially towards a group and whispered, 'They are saying that a Caley man is getting the job!'

CHAPTER TEN

A PASSION FOR RAILWAYS

A PASSION FOR railways is as old as the eulogies by the actress Fanny Kemble about the experience of riding on the footplate with George Stephenson before the opening of the Liverpool & Manchester Railway in 1830. Her descriptions of the steam locomotive and the sensation of travelling at unprecedented speed were among the first to try to capture the unique appeal of railways. That appeal is so multi-faceted that there are innumerable specialists, ranging from the student of locomotive performance to the admirer of railway architecture, from the expert on signalling systems to a devotee of anything to do with the railways of Peru. A prodigious body of information has been built up over the past two centuries, mainly in books and such long-running magazines as the UK's *Railway Magazine*, which first appeared in July 1897, and the 1940-established *Trains* in the US. Millions of photographs have been taken, from the early glass-plate records of the mid 19th century to the final days of steam in China and Cuba. For those of a certain age, it was the fascination of the steam locomotive and the atmosphere of the steam railway which drew them into the wider subject, though younger generations have found an appeal in subsequent forms of traction. Many who don't count themselves as railway buffs but just like trains warm to the poetry of John Betjeman, enjoy the railway settings of Andrew Martin's crime novels and would wander down to the railway to watch a steam-hauled excursion pass by.

NO MILE UNTRAVELLED

The first and probably only person to travel every mile of track traversed by scheduled passenger train in the British Isles was a chemist from Henley-in-Arden in Warwickshire named Thomas Richard Perkins. It took him nearly 60 years to accomplish his goal, beginning in the 1870s around his native district of Kidderminster. He completed England, Wales and Scotland in 1928 at Tonteg, where a new connection had been put in between the Barry and Taff Vales lines, and Ireland on a day in 1932 when he alighted at Athboy in County Meath. During those years he published articles about byways that had particularly appealed to him, but there was no fanfare for this personal goal. He was the antithesis of what some today call a 'track basher'; as his writings showed, he took a profound interest in the history and architecture of the places he visited.

ENCOUNTER AT KLAMATH FALLS

One of the legendary railway buffs in the US was Rogers E.M. Whitaker (1900–81), better known to some by his pen name of E.M. Frimbo. After working at the *New York Times* and sharing a theatrical boarding house with Mae West, he went to the *New Yorker* where he spent most of his working life as an editor. His love of train travel led to him clocking up 2.7 million miles on the rails, leaving the office on a Friday night to travel to some previously unexplored byway of the network. He disliked cars: 'A car is a rolling sneeze, a slice of selfishness,' he wrote, whereas train travel can be 'the most nearly perfect way of moving from one place to another'.

He was also fond of jazz, and these passions came together one night at Klamath Falls in Oregon on the Southern Pacific. He had arrived by the *Caribou Special* and was armed with an engine pass authorising him to travel on a freight leaving Klamath Falls at 5pm. Kicking his heels awaiting departure time, Whitaker was standing where the Pullman car of a northbound train from Oakland to Portland drew to a halt. Off stepped the jazz pianist Fats Waller.

'Mr Frimbo,' exclaimed Waller, 'what the hell are you doing here?'

'Mr Waller,' he replied, 'what the hell are *you* doing here?'

'I've got the band with me. We're playing a gig in Klamath Falls tonight.'

'I'm taking an overnight freight train to California.'

'Man, you're crazier than any of my musicians.'

DRIVING INSTRUCTION

For decades Cambridge University has had a thriving Railway Club, which used to hold its annual dinner in a restaurant car between Liverpool Street and Cambridge. During the 1950s, in the days before the substitution of common sense by 'health & safety', the Society was allowed a 'driver instruction train' between Linton and Haverhill on the now-closed Cambridge–Marks Tey line. There were no Sunday trains on the line, so a former Great Eastern Railway 2–4–0 and two coaches were provided for the students to be taught the rudiments of driving a steam locomotive.

DVORAK AND RAILWAYS

After music, railways were Dvorak's great interest. He grew up in Nelahozeves, about 15 miles (25 km) north of Prague, at a time when the railway and a nearby tunnel were being built by Italian workers. It is said that in the evening some of them would gather at the shop owned by Dvorak's father, who was very fond of music, and sing their songs, providing a novel influence on the embryonic composer.

Later in life, when living in the Czech capital, he would visit stations in the course of his early morning walk and knew the locomotive drivers personally. During a lacklustre concert, Dvorak would prefer to slip out and watch the departure of an international express at Franz Joseph I station, now Prague's main station. On one occasion, he was too busy to go to the station, so he asked his future son-in-law Josef Suk to note down the locomotive number on the afternoon Prague–Přibram train. When the young man returned with the tender number, Dvorak pretended to be cross and asked his daughter, 'How can you expect me to let you marry a young man with so little sense of responsibility?'

During his years in the US he relished a train journey from New York to Chicago, and particularly enjoyed locomotive changing points such as Philadelphia, Harrisburg and Pittsburgh.

FOUR-LEGGED FRIENDS

During the late 1940s and early '50s the stationmaster at Eridge in Surrey had a Welsh Collie named Prince who was partial to riding on the footplate. The dog would race along the platforms whenever a branch train came in and assume a begging position, which no crew could resist.

It was a chill caught while visiting the main locomotive depot in Prague during wintry weather that hastened his death in May 1904.

THE FIRST RAILWAY PHOTOGRAPH

It is impossible to be dogmatic about the date of the first railway photograph. Certainly a Calotype was taken in 1851 of the South Eastern Railway Crampton 4–2–0 No. 134 *Folkestone* at the Great Exhibition in Hyde Park. However, there is a photograph of a Taff Vale Railway 0–6–0 *Newbridge*, built in 1846 by Hick, Hargreaves & Co. of Bolton in Lancashire, with the date 1849 on the back of an original print.

MRS MALLOWAN'S TRAVELS

In 1930 the writer of crime novels Agatha Christie married the archaeologist Max Mallowan. She joined him on many of his digs in Iraq, travelling across Europe by such trains as the Orient Express and the Taurus Express. These journeys were anything but an ordeal to her: 'Dear Victoria, gateway to the world beyond England. How I love your continental platform, and how I love trains anyway. Snuffing up the sulphurous smell ecstatically, so different from the faint, aloof, distantly oily smell of a boat. But a train, a big snorting hurrying, companionable train with its big puffing engine, sending up clouds of steam and seeming to say impatiently, "I've got to be off, I've got to be off", is a friend.' She famously used these journeys to create the background for *Murder on the Orient Express*, written in the Pera Palace Hotel in Istanbul, where a room is preserved as a memorial to her visits.

PLUS ÇA CHANGE . . .

In encouraging visitors to see the Furness Railway display of photographs at the 1910 Anglo-Japanese Exhibition at White City, the *Railway & Travel Monthly* commented: 'It ought to do much to convince the holidaymaker that there is no reason why he should spend all his money in foreign countries nor on foreign railways, for of its kind there is no scenery that can compare with that to which the Furness Railway gives access.'

STIRRING UP OXFORD

'Passion' is probably not the word most people would use in describing Colonel T.E. Lawrence's relationship with railways, but a reminder of his time sabotaging Turkish supply lines in Palestine was brought back to England. He kept in his college rooms at All Souls, Oxford, where he had been awarded a seven-year Fellowship, the station bell from Tel Shahm, 340 miles (545 km) from Damascus. He captured the souvenir on 19 April 1918, when a dawn attack on the station with a Bedouin contingent succeeded in surprising the Turkish troops, who surrendered without a fight. Lawrence claimed the bell, while others took the ticket punch and office stamp. Seats on wartime Hejaz Railway trains were priced according to their distance from the locomotive, the cheapest being right behind the locomotive.

Robert Graves recalls a day when he saw from the Radcliffe Camera a small crimson Hejaz flag fluttering from the All Souls flagpole, and another when Lawrence rang the station bell from his window into the Quadrangle. When Graves suggested he'd wake the whole college, Lawrence replied, 'It needs waking up.'

MISS POTTER ON HOLIDAY

Besides regular visits to the Lake District, the family of Beatrix Potter would often take a house near Dunkeld in the Highlands of Scotland. It stood close enough to the Highland Railway's Perth–Inverness main line for her to watch the trains pass, and she wrote: 'To my mind there is scarcely a more splendid beast in the world than a large Locomotive ... I cannot imagine a finer sight than the Express, with two engines, rushing down this incline [from Kingswood Tunnel].'

PASS THE PORT – BY RAIL

Several Indian maharajahs owned their own public railways and even more had luxurious private railway carriages for their journeys, but the Maharaja Jaiaja Rao Scindia of Gwalior also had a railway built around the dining-table of the Jai Vilas Palace. Made of silver, the respectable representation of a 4–4–0 circulated crystal decanters, nuts and cigars in its train of wagons passing in front of guests. As soon as a decanter was lifted, the train stopped. It was created for the colossal palace built in expectation of the 1875–6 visit to India of the Prince of Wales. The Maharajah was apparently cautious by nature (except in his building projects) and he had the ability to override a halt and take the alcohol beyond the reach of someone he felt had already had enough. The story goes that a malfunction on the great night toppled the port decanter into the Prince's lap.

GWALIOR LIGHT RAILWAY

The Maharajah's son, Madhav Rao Scindia, who succeeded in 1886, had developed a more practical love of railways and things mechanical under his British tutor, J.W. Johnstone. He built a 2 ft gauge system within the palace grounds at Gwalior and extensions to the Residency at Morar, the state farm and a shooting box at Sussera. The Maharajah enjoyed driving the railway's second locomotive, a Kerr Stuart 4–4–0 built in Stoke-on-Trent, and it is said that it was fired on sandalwood and used jasmine oil for lubrication. Strictly speaking, this railway contravened the British intention of retaining powers of railway construction, but since the Maharajah's enthusiasm was the result of his distinctly British education, they accepted it and even allowed the railway's gradual expansion into a system of 250 miles (400 km), with lines to Bhind, Shivpuri and Sheopur Kalan. The ultimate seal of approval was given by the Viceroy, Lord Curzon, who opened the first two lines in 1899. H.F. Prevost Battersby, a British journalist accompanying the Prince of Wales during his 1903 visit, was amazed by Scindia's ability 'to drive car and locomotive or strip the works of either, as skilfully as a chauffeur or an engineer'.

WHAT'S IN A NAME?

The delightfully named Leicestershire station of John O'Gaunt had nothing to do with the fourth son of Edward III; it took its name from a fox covert and replaced the station's previous name of Burrow & Twyford, the villages it served, in 1883, doubtless to please the hunting fraternity that brought hunt specials to the line.

THE BEST JOB IN THE WORLD?

Railway photographers must envy the life led by Nicholas Morant, who became the official photographer of the Canadian Pacific Railway in 1939. He had *carte blanche* to operate as he saw fit providing he came up with the results needed. Part of his *modus operandi* was to have a specially fitted-out caboose shunted into a siding near a shot he wanted and wait until he got exactly the right light. This caboose might be home for days, even weeks, for Nick Morant and his wife.

But photography in the Canadian wilderness is not without its dangers, and not long after his appointment, Morant was near Sherbrooke Lake in British Columbia with a Swiss guide, Christian Haesler, when they ran into the worst possible danger – a female grizzly with cub. The guide was badly mauled and Morant jumped down from the tree in which he'd taken refuge and attacked the bear with a long fir pole. It saved Haesler, but Morant was seriously injured. They lost contact but Morant was found 10 hours later by a Royal Canadian Mounted Police constable and his Newfoundland dog.

CANADIAN PACIFIC RAILWAY

FOUR-LEGGED FRIENDS

A signalman at Field in British Columbia had a dog that accompanied him on the maintenance trolleys up the spiral tunnels towards Kicking Horse Pass, but the dog hated the tunnels so he would leap off and race up the hill to the upper portal and leap on again.

THOMAS AND FRIENDS

A love of trains has been engendered in millions of children by the Thomas the Tank Engine stories of the Rev Wilbert Awdry (1911–97). They developed from the stories Awdry told his son Christopher while the boy was confined to bed with measles in 1942 at King's Norton in Birmingham. Awdry's wife encouraged him to submit them for publication. The small landscape format chosen by the publisher Edmund Ward for the first book in 1945 was crucial to their success – over 50 million copies had been sold by the time of Awdry's death. The morality tale adventures were usually based on a true event, and had to be 'true to life' in railway terms. A wider audience was reached when the stories were adapted for television with Beatle Ringo Starr as the narrator.

TREASURE IN A TIMETABLE

In the 1970s a man bought a box of second-hand books from a north London shop, including a railway timetable, and for the next thirty years he was puzzled by eight small etchings he found inside it. He first thought that the powerful visions of men being stripped of flesh or drowning were facsimiles. But in 2007 he took them to the Tate Gallery, where they were identified as original William Blake etchings, probably done for the series of books produced by his method of 'illuminated printing'. The hand-coloured prints were bought by the Tate for £441,000 and went on display in July 2010.

SAVIOUR OF LOST CAUSES

One of the most idiosyncratic figures of the railway world during the late 19th and early 20th centuries was Lieutenant-Colonel Holman Frederick Stephens (1868–1931). An engineer by training, he was entrusted with his first construction assignment at just 22, building the Paddock Wood–Hawkhurst line with an economy that would characterise his later projects. Using the provisions of the Light Railways Act of 1896, Stephens became involved with a large portfolio of minor impecunious railways, variously as engineer, locomotive superintendent and managing director, as well as acquiring major shareholdings in some of them. The best-known railways with which he held posts are the Kent & East Sussex Railway and the Festiniog and Welsh Highland railways.

His management style was equally idiosyncratic. Behind a disciplinarian approach lay a paternalism that has gone out of fashion. Visits would be unannounced, an inspection train would be rustled up and he would tour the line handing out cigars or coins to favoured staff. This would be followed by a salvo of terse memos calling for deficiencies to be rectified. His other great interest was classical mythology, reflected in the names bestowed on locomotives that were as ungodlike as mechanically possible.

Even the advertising devised at his headquarters in Tonbridge, Kent, was eccentric. Passengers were urged to 'support the local line' by travelling 'across country away from the dusty and crowded roads on home-made steel instead of on imported rubber'.

COMPANY LOYALTY

It is hard from our perspective to imagine the feelings of loyalty that railway companies once engendered. The service tradition generally fostered a sense of pride in the job, but there was also fierce loyalty to one's company. When the 14-year-old Felix Pole travelled from Marlborough to Swindon for an interview with the Great Western Railway in 1891, he scored marks for taking a longer way round by GWR rather than a direct route on the Midland & South Western Junction Railway (Pole was to become General Manager of the GWR and receive a knighthood).

FILMING *THE RAILWAY CHILDREN*

The actor and director Lionel Jeffries used an unorthodox way to film the scene where the three children narrowly manage to stop the train following a landslide and Roberta faints on the track. As they flagged it down, he got the young actors to shout 'Pots! Pots!' as the train backed away from them – and simply reversed the film in editing.

A PASSION FOR BRITAIN

S.P.B. Mais (1885–1975) had a passion for using railways, if not for the railways themselves, and his name is inseparable from the publications of the Great Western and Southern railways between the wars. He wrote so many books – over 200 – about topography, local history and particularly walks from stations that Churchill once remarked that the pace of Mais's output made him feel tired.

Born in Birmingham, Stuart Petre Brodie Mais grew up in Derbyshire and after graduating from Christ Church, Oxford, he taught until he joined the *Oxford Mail* and then Fleet Street and became a broadcaster for the BBC. He pre-empted Alistair Cooke by broadcasting *Letter from America* from 1933; Cooke's *American Letter* began in 1946, becoming *Letter from America* in 1950. Mais also broadcast *Kitchen Front* (sometimes featuring Marguerite Patten), *Microphone at Large* and *This Unknown Island*, making his voice one of the most recognised in Britain.

Mais was an ardent campaigner for, and celebrator of, the English countryside and traditions in the mould of Clough Williams-Ellis and J.B. Priestley. But writing was no more lucrative then than now, and his wife once recalled having to hand over the contents of her piggybank to a pressing creditor.

GRAND TRUNK RAILWAY SYSTEM

RAILWAY COMPANIES MENTIONED

BCR	Bishop's Castle Railway
CIWL	Compagnie Internationale des Wagons-Lits et des Grands Express Européens (the International Sleeping Car Company)
CNR	Canadian National Railway
CPR	Canadian Pacific Railway
D&RG	Denver & Rio Grande, USA
ELR	East Lancashire Railway
FR	Ffestiniog Railway
GER	Great Eastern Railway
GJR	Grand Junction Railway
GNR	Great Northern Railway
GNSR	Great North of Scotland Railway
GTR	Grand Trunk Railway, Canada
GWR	Great Western Railway
HR	Highland Railway
LBSCR	London Brighton & South Coast Railway
LMR	Liverpool & Manchester Railway
LMS	London Midland & Scottish Railway
LNER	London & North Eastern Railway
LNWR	London & North Western Railway
LSWR	London & South Western Railway
LYR	Lancashire & Yorkshire Railway
MR	Midland Railway
NER	North Eastern Railway
OWW	Oxford, Worcester & Wolverhampton Railway
S&D	Stockton & Darlington Railway
SNCF	Société Nationale des Chemins de Fer, France
VoR	Vale of Rheidol Railway

BIBLIOGRAPHY

BOOKS

Bagwell, Philip S. *The Railwaymen* (George Allen & Unwin, 1963)

Barrie, D.S.M. *Regional History of the Railways of Great Britain: South Wales* (David & Charles, 1980)

Baxter, Antony. *The Two Foot Gauge Enigma* (Plateway Press, 1998)

Baxter, Bertram. *Stone Blocks and Iron Rails* (David & Charles, 1966)

Biddle, Gordon. *The Railway Surveyors* (Ian Allan, 1990)

Carter, Oliver. *British Railway Hotels* (Silver Link, 1990)

Coleman, Terry. *The Railway Navvies* (Hutchinson, 1965)

Croxton, Anthony H. *Railways of Zimbabwe* (David & Charles, 1982)

de Courtais, Nicholas. *The New Radnor Branch* (Wild Swan, 1992)

Dow, Andrew. *Dow's Dictionary of Railway Quotations* (John Hopkins University Press, 2006)

Dunn, J.M. *Reflections on a Railway Career* (Ian Allan, 1966)

Faith, Nicholas. *The World the Railways Made* (Bodley Head, 1990)

Fawcett, Dick. *Ganger, Guard and Signalman* (Bradford Barton, 1981)

Ferneyhough, Frank. *Steam Up!* (Robert Hale, 1983)

Fletcher, Malcolm, and Taylor, John. *Railways: The Pioneer Years* (Studio Editions, 1990)

Freeman, Michael. *Railways and the Victorian Imagination* (Yale University Press, 1999)

Graves, Robert. *Goodbye to All That* (Jonathan Cape, 1929)

Green, C.C. *The Vale of Rheidol* (Wild Swan, 1986)

Haresnape, Brian. *Pullman: Travelling in Style* (Ian Allan, 1987)

Holden, Bryan. *The Long Haul: the Life and Times of the Railway Horse* (J.A. Allen, 1985)

Hughes, Gervase. *Dvořák* (Cassell, 1867)

Jordan, Arthur & Elisabeth. *Away for the Day* (Silver Link, 1991)

Lambert, Anthony J. *Nineteenth Century Railway History through the Illustrated London News* (David & Charles, 1984)
Lowe, James W. *British Steam Locomotive Builders* (Guild Publishing, 1975)
McDermot, E.T. *History of the Great Western Railway* (Ian Allan, 1964)
Mellentin, Julian. *Kendal and Windermere Railway* (Dalesman, 1980)
Morgan, Bryan. *The End of the Line* (Cleaver Hume, 1955)
Morgan, Bryan (ed.). *The Great Trains* (Edita, 1973)
Nicholson, James. *The Hejaz Railway* (Stacey International, 2005)
Nock, O.S. *The Highland Railway* (Ian Allan, 1965)
Page, Martin. *The Lost Pleasures of the Great Trains* (Weidenfeld & Nicolson, 1975)
Pearson, Michael. *The Sealed Train* (Macmillan, 1975)
Peaty, Ian R. *Brewery Railways* (David & Charles, 1985)
Pole, Graeme. *The Spiral Tunnels and the Big Hill* (Mountain Vision, 2009)
Robbins, Michael. *Points and Signals* (George Allen & Unwin, 1967)
Roche, T.W.E. *The Withered Arm* (West Country Handbooks, 1967)
Rolt, L.T.C. *George and Robert Stephenson* (Longmans, 1960)
Rolt, L.T.C. *Red for Danger: The Classic History of British Railways* (The History Press, 2009)
Ross, David. *The Highland Railway* (Tempus, 2005)
Scindia, Vijayaraje. *Princess* (Century Hutchinson, 1985)
Simmons, Jack (ed.). *Railways: An Anthology* (Collins, 1991)
Simmons, Jack, and Biddle, Gordon. *The Oxford Companion to British Railway History* (OUP, 1997)
Smith, David L. *Tales of the Glasgow & South Western Railway* (Ian Allan, 1962)
Smith, Martin. *British Railway Bridges & Viaducts* (Ian Allan, 1994)
Smith, William H. *The Bromyard Branch* (Kidderminster Railway Museum, 1998)
Thomas, John. *The Skye Railway* (David & Charles, 1977)
Thomas, John. *The West Highland Railway* (David & Charles, 1965)
Torr, Cecil. *Small Talk at Wreyland* (Cambridge University Press, 1918–23)
Whitaker, Rogers E.M., and Hiss, Anthony. *All Aboard with E.M. Frimbo* (André Deutsch, 1975)

Wilson, Roger Burdett. *Go Great Western* (David & Charles, 1970)
Wolmar, Christian. *The Subterranean Railway* (Atlantic, 2004)
Wooler, Neil. *Dinner in the Diner* (David & Charles, 1987)

PERIODICALS

Back Track
British Railway Journal
Chime
Highland Railway Journal
Industrial Archaeology News
Railway & Travel Monthly
Railway Archive
Railway Magazine
Railway World
SLS Journal
Steam Days
Trains Illustrated

In addition, personal memories recorded in local archives and museums have been used.

INDEX

ACKNOWLEDGEMENTS

I am most grateful to the following for suggestions, sources and help with checking facts: Margaret Baxter, Gordon Biddle, Monty Brown, Barry Doe, Michael Dunn, Keith Fenwick, Dr Ann Glen, Andrew Hine, Sarah Hine, John Knowles, Robin Leleux, Peter Lemmey, Bob Meanley, David Postle, John Ross, Paul Shannon, Peter Thorpe, George Toms, Michael Whitehouse, Angela Whiteway and Julian Worth. Particular thanks to Dr Pete Waterman for his kind endorsement of the book, coming from someone who has done so much for the appreciation and conservation of our railway heritage. I would also like to thank the staff of Kidderminster Railway Museum, the London Library and the National Railway Museum for their kind assistance.

My thanks to Carey Smith and Samantha Smith at Ebury for their encouragement and exemplary skills at handling authors, which from the author's recollection of his time as a commissioning editor sometimes seems like herding cats.